ROMAN RULE
The Eternal Empire

Melvin Pugh

authorHOUSE®

AuthorHouse™
1663 Liberty Drive
Bloomington, IN 47403
www.authorhouse.com
Phone: 1-800-839-8640

First published by AuthorHouse   10/25/0011

ISBN: 978-1-4670-3851-5 (sc)
ISBN: 978-1-4670-3850-8 (hc)
ISBN: 978-1-4670-3849-2 (e)

Library of Congress Control Number: 2011916881

Printed in the United States of America

To Mary F. Pugh, a special lady and phenomenal mother to all of her children. *"Thanks for your Love Mom"*

Contents

INTRODUCTION

My inquisitive nature compelled me to research and explore the remote parallels of the late Roman Empire and the empire of the United States. I am convinced that these two seemingly divergent world powers share a mystical bond, with the Roman Empire continuing to project latent influences on America and the world. I first became captivated by the subtle hints and definitive connections between the late empire and the current American empire at a young age, and as I grew to adulthood, the premise beckoned and taunted me for over 20 years. Rome dominated the known world for, by various estimates, 700 to 800 years and was on the field of imperialism for 1000 years.

It was Rome that was at the height of power when the birth of Jesus Christ heralded the arrival of a previously foretold Messiah. Nearly 2000 years later, the United States was instrumental in the birth of the nation of Israel on May 14, 1948. The U.S. had recently become the foremost world power with the victory of World War II; this was achieved through the unleashing of the first atomic bomb. These two epochal events were predicted in an ancient prophetic book long before the conception of America. The profound nature of these events, speaks to the premise of each being preternaturally related based on the effects they have had on civilization worldwide. The prophecy, related to Israel, definitively predicted the inception of its sovereignty centuries before it happened. The discovery of the Dead Sea Scrolls in 1947, and the information contained therein, is further corroborating evidence of the significance of Israel as a sovereign nation. Based on the outcomes of three wars, with Israel as the assailed nation, there are evidently supernatural forces at work. These

1

same forces bind the United States to the children of God and the Judeo Christian Bible.

On the periphery we find the United States emulating the late Roman Empire as an Imperial power. The adoption of the Roman form of government, religion(s), social mores, and the hybrid structures of the *Republic* are striking and irrefutable. In order to understand the true nature of America, its identity, and its future, it is important to fully comprehend the latent yet powerful influences that are projected in and throughout the Unites States.

In this work, I examine the origins of what truly makes America unique and universal, all in one entropic cauldron. There are conflicting ambiguities, and be advised, this is by design. If you are truly honest with yourself you know that in human nature we are wired for contradiction. How we allow ourselves to be entertained by evil while professing goodness. How there really is a thin line between love and hate and we vary the thickness of that line to suit our consciousness on a given day. Our progenitors used some of these same drives to forge empires and to instill in their progeny an evolutionary derived hunger to build and destroy with cyclic certainty.

DRUGSTORE 9000

The current health-care reform initiatives and attendant controversies of the United States speak to the complex moral questions related to the underlying motives of those who have money and those that do not. The exorbitant medical carousel is indeed driven by phenomenal profit for— but not limited to—medical equipment manufacturers, pharmaceutical companies, insurance companies, and the Hippocratic Oath attendants--- also known as doctors. In the most powerful country extant on this planet, we find things are not as they seem; perhaps this is intended in the quest to live a reasonable life, as free from illness as possible, with a good death, and somewhere on the high side of the average U.S. life-span. Vanity or perhaps feigned indifference may bring a brief moment of comfort, but make no mistake; the escape is temporary at best, as we are all destined to face the reality of money, politics, conflict, worry, sickness, and ultimately the final call.

There are those in government who blame the high cost of health-care on waste, duplication, fraud, and of course, greed. Most of these same individuals are very good at identifying the problems in the system but become eerily reticent in offering effective solutions to the various problems that plague the American medical-monopoly. The "medical arts" are intended to be as arcane and dogmatically complex as humanly possible, with the answer to the mystery being locked in a word known simply as mortality. For many, this encompasses the totality of life existence in our fragile, electro-chemical, carbon-based vessel that we sometimes abuse but always rely on as the only true home for our most cherished possession. Here lies the essence of being; the government and the medical industry know that regardless of individual station, no other issue fully encompasses the life cycle. By virtue of biogenic and geopolitical intricacy, the powers-that-be control a significant aspect of all humanity and untold wealth.

Medicine, by virtue of its nature, is not an exact science; this is perhaps the most compelling component of the curiosity that motivates the physician in the healing art. This premise is directly attributed to the father of medicine, Hippocrates (460-377 B.C.). After nearly 2500 years, the "Hippocrati" and their subsequent descendents are credited with handing down many of the best practices or "dogma" related to the healing arts. Also known as "dogmatici" (dogmatics), these early physicians, of Greek origin, included Thessalus and Polybus; through their practice and teaching, they were instrumental in influencing their Roman conquerors in the adoption of structured medical practice, during the period of 400 B.C. From this era, and for at least seven centuries, the best practicing physicians were of the Roman Empire. The incessant wars perpetuated by the Romans contributed to advancements in surgery that were practiced in the first "MASH" units developed under Marius, one of Rome's fiercest warriors and most revered generals. (1)

By the 2nd century A.D., Rome had produced not only noteworthy physicians but also major medical-arts practices still utilized in modern medicine; these include the sterilization of surgical tools in boiling water and using fresh utensils for each patient. Aulus Cornelius Celsus is considered to be one of the principal medical adherents to detailed records in procedure and practice of the healing arts. Historians call his record, *The Eight Books of Medicine,* the most comprehensive detailed description of surgical procedures ever produced by a Roman writer. (2) In these writings Celsus formulated and promoted the principle that "accurate diagnosis must precede treatment." The prolific writings of Celsus could also be considered the forerunner of the "charting" prevalent in medicine today. It was during the reign of Emperor Augustus that the first Roman medical organization was formed, and history suggests that Celsus was the catalyst in its creation.

Galen holds the distinction as the most renowned doctor of antiquity and, although technically from Greece, he is considered the principal doctor of Rome. Galen also promoted the discipline of record-keeping and distinguished his medical practice by the use of drugs, such as opium, during surgery. It was Rome, and its avant-garde (for the times) approach, that developed the first hospitals for observation and dedicated rest and recuperation. By 164 A.D., Greco-Roman medicine had advanced to include specialization among physicians, including interns, urologists, ophthalmologists and thoracic surgeons. One of the most compelling aspects of medicine in antiquity is the fact that there were some good doctors and some very bad. Only the rich members of the aristocracy obtained the services of the best doctors; obviously the doctors that were near or equal to Galen were reserved, and the plebeians (low members) of society received mediocre doctors and treatment—which tends to mirror, to some degree, modern times.

There is any number of speculative reasons why medicine and the healing-arts in general drifted into abeyance during the Middle Ages. After the fall of Rome, the early Middle Ages, also called the Dark Ages, were a time of rampant paganism and necromancy. This environment bred medical indifference among vast numbers of warring factions, tribes, sub-cultures and even the detached pockets of Christians. With "black magic" as comfort and superstition as a guiding principle, who needs a doctor? Centuries passed before the Age of Enlightenment heralded the serious establishment of medicine as a science and a business.

In England, it was Henry VIII in 1518 that formalized and founded the Royal College of Physicians. This group of doctors went on to establish the first rules governing all aspects of the medical-arts at that time, including a defined charter by 1540 and a special "Quacks" charter in 1542. In 1617, the Society of Apothecaries was also formed in England.

By 1832, The British Medical Association (BMA) had been formed; this would later be the model for creating a similar association in America—which could be considered the beginning of the medical-monopoly that exists today. (3) In the period from 1700 to the early days of the BMA, the notable inventions of nitrous-oxide (laughing gas) by chemist Sir Humphrey Davy gave doctors a new more versatile anesthetic. His apprentice, the brilliant scientist Michael Faraday, continued his work and ultimately Faraday became famous in his own right. With the refinement of morphine from opium in 1804, the physician now had two highly effective anesthetics, (besides the opium) which contributed to advancements in surgery.

Morphine was extensively used during the American Civil War and was administered with a newly developed device we know as the hypodermic syringe. Not until 1853 was there a fine-needle, capable of easily piercing the skin, developed and mass-produced. This medical turning point, the ability to administer a broad spectrum of medicines without the problems associated with the digestive system, allowed doctors to use less medicine with quick-acting results but also purportedly led to "soldier's disease" and a high incidence of morphine addiction.

The American Medical Association was officially founded in 1847, and although there were some successful physicians at the time, it would be 30 years before medical licensing and the purging of "irregular practitioners" (quacks) made the agency respectable. (4) From the outset, the leadership aggressively set out to consolidate its dominance in medicine. In identifying the influence of the medical schools over the hospitals and the medical examination boards over the medical schools, the AMA sought and eventually gained control over the various state medical examination boards. The AMA began rewriting licensing laws, as well as the medical school curricula. The number of schools began to decline, along with the number of doctors; this was the start of the AMA imperative, and the remaining doctors' salaries and prestige began to rise dramatically.

With the American Medical Association in firm control of health-care at the start of the twentieth century, a new paradigm for medicine, doctors, hospitals, insurance coverage and a quasi-control of government began to emerge. The first order of business, more money in the doctor's pocket, had effectively been established with control of the licensing and review boards. The head of the AMA, Dr. George H. Simmons, created the culture of the AMA being the absolute arbiter of all things pertaining to medicine. Dr. Simmons came up with the idea of publishing the *Journal of the American Medical Association*, with the expressed intent of gaining advertising revenue and giving the "seal of approval" to select drug companies. This was a brilliant business initiative and by 1909, *JAMA* was generating revenues of $150,000 per year. In addition, its subscriber ranks grew from 8,000 in 1900 to more than 70,000 in 1910. (5) Having your product endorsed by the AMA proved to be very lucrative for all concerned; and although there were controversies pertaining to extortion and unethical business practices, Dr. Simmons relentlessly pursued and established AMA preeminence in the world of medicine.

Dr. Simmons was pro-active in finding a suitable second-in-command, and ultimate successor, in Dr. Morris Fishbein. By 1924, the multiple scandals associated with Dr. Simmons forced his resignation and heralded the ascendancy of Dr, Fishbein. What his predecessor might have lacked, Dr. Fishbein more than compensated for with an aggressive business model that made Dr. Simmons look like a Boy Scout. Dr. Fishbein wrote derisive books and attacked all forms of competition with assiduous conviction. The competing health doctrine, known as homeopathy, was excoriated and given the moniker of "cult." Fishbein attacked "health fraud" in multiple media, including syndicated newspapers and his own weekly radio show heard by millions of Americans; this was during a time when radio had profound cultural influence. There were occasions where Dr. Fishbein attempted to buy promising health-care treatments and apparatus; if the perspective owner refused to sell the rights, the individual was attacked, derided, and ultimately destroyed. If the individual was a doctor, he was labeled a "quack" and punished through AMA channels; if the person was a layman, Dr. Fishbein would have the individual arrested for practicing without a license or have the product confiscated by the Food and Drug Administration (FDA) or the Federal Trade Commission (FTC). (6) The first evidence of medical tyranny reared its ugly head, and you did not want Dr. Morris Fishbein as an enemy.

These abuses caught up with Dr. Fishbein in 1937, as he and the AMA were tried and convicted of anti-trust violations for conspiracy and restraint of trade. But a huge bank account does wonders, as Dr. Fishbein—and the AMA—rebounded and, with the help of a new ally, grew exponentially more powerful. That new partner in commerce was the tobacco companies—Camel and L&M in particular. By 1950, JAMA was making in excess of $10 million dollars in advertising revenue annually from the tobacco companies alone. Like his predecessor, Dr. Fishbein was eventually forced out in 1949; but unlike his mentor, he picked up a high-paying consulting job with one of the tobacco companies that he had helped to grow market share and profit.

By the decade of the 1960s, the AMA had established its organization among all the monolithic power brokers in the capitalistic realm, the operative word being capital---and more money. The AMA, starting in 1927, had stopped, modified, influenced, or outright controlled most of the legislation related to health-insurance adoption and had become adept at molding the rules of the game to suit its growing cupidity. The Medicare bill of 1965 is one of the most definitive examples of the AMA taking a government program intended to help the aged and, by using advanced undermining techniques, turning the program into a taxpayer-funded channel of largess to the members of the AMA. This was (is) done through creative billing practices and lobbying law makers for exemptions and special concessions intended to covertly fleece the Federal Government (the people) by stealth. (7) Through high-powered lobbying and the blandishment of commission members, the AMA was able to alter pay schedules to the benefit of the doctors, make medical malpractice lawsuits (which encourage defensive medicine) harder to file, and completely protect doctors from anti-trust litigation. The fee-for-service aspect of Medicare billing monetarily encouraged doctors to perform more services; when Medicare froze fees; the doctors simply ordered more patient visits and medical tests.

The American Medical Political Action Committee (AMPAC) is perhaps the most powerful PAC in the United States. Its power stems from the relentless campaigns to get "their" men in positions of power and the philosophy of "socioeconomics." The AMA is further augmented by the joining of forces with the equally powerful Pharmaceutical Manufacturers Association (PMA). Through the combined wealth of the AMA and the PMA, the possibilities of monopolistic and anti-trust activity are beyond the imagination of the average layman. In 1974, Congress sought to pass comprehensive campaign reform in an attempt to attenuate the power of the AMA-PMA. It was a study in futility. In 1976 Congress added amendments to the 1974 campaign act, but again the AMA-PMA found loopholes in the laws and were able to get their candidates all the money they needed—nearly $1 million—to run in an election cycle. (8)

There are hundreds of examples of abuse of power in the American Medical Association and their ubiquitous partner, the PMA (big pharmaceutical) companies. In the last 40 years, the symbiotic relationship between the AMA and the PMA has combined to form a medical oligarchy. During the early days, the AMA was the dominant partner in the ascendancy to the position of power now held by the medical-monopoly. With advances in technology and pharmacology, big pharmaceutical companies have now taken the lead, in an apparent "tail wagging the dog" reversal of fortune. This is not to say that doctors, or the AMA, have been relegated to second-class by any measure. The AMA still contributes to the success of the drug companies by assisting or conducting clinical trials and endorsing the use and proliferation of various drugs. (Note the eagerness of doctors to give out samples of drugs to their patients). This is not magnanimity, but shrewdly crafted advertisement and the quest to get patients hooked on the new drug; ultimately perpetuating sales and profits for the drug companies. (Note the prodigious spending and promotion of various drugs by the drug companies in television advertisements).

The advent of laws (patent limiting) pertaining to the original drug versus generic (cheaper) drugs being allowed to compete in the market place, may have weakened some of the larger drug companies to some degree. This has apparently contributed to the top drug companies merging and forming mega-drug-companies to maintain their supremacy. In 2009 alone, drug company Pfizer purchased Wyeth for $68 billion dollars, making the combined units the largest single drug maker on the planet. (9) Just six weeks later, Merck purchased Schering-Plough to become the second-largest drug manufacturer. In both mergers the purchasing company cited the need to combat competition from generic drug makers and price. (10)

Drug makers contribute to the challenges associated with health-care reform and are thus characterized as the greedy and demonic chemical peddlers. Some of this derision is justified. However, if the average person knew of the complexity, time, and billions of dollars associated with the development of certain drugs, not to mention intellectual property rights, they too would want to recoup their investment and enjoy some of the profit and spoils contributing to a "better life through chemistry." The drug makers have created a need for their products—in some cases—by making drugs that were later determined to have caused medical maladies, thus perpetrating a further need for a "miracle" cure and an additional, irrefutable purpose for the pharmaceutical industry.

One example of this relates to vaccines. Vaccination has been integral to medicine for over two centuries, dating from Edward Jenner and his smallpox vaccine (1796). The early success Jenner experienced contributed to the founding of immunological medical-science and an improvement in the human condition. But, like all scientific advancement, there are associated controversy and risks.

The era of the first polio vaccine (1954) and famed epidemiologist Jonas Salk speaks to a period when the Salk vaccine was the panacea for the scourge of the crippling poliomyelitis. Because of the tremendous fear of being paralyzed by polio, any successful preparation that gave hope was accepted without question. For the most part, Dr. Salk and others made a tremendous contribution to the eradication of polio in the twentieth century. Polio became a polarizing issue with respect to research credit, politics, money, and ultimately fame. John Enders received a Nobel Prize for his discovery of how to grow the constituent parts of the polio virus in a laboratory setting; it was Salk, however, that advanced the use of inactivated virus in the making of a usable vaccine. (11) Dr. Salk took much of the credit for the vaccine and may have even disparaged a colleague-turned-enemy in one, Albert Sabin. The story is well chronicled and even includes Communist Russia as an aside. It would be interesting to find parallels in the career of Galen.

The plot dramatically changes course when, some years later, Dr. Bernice Eddy took the initiative to test monkey kidney cell extracts for cancer-causing agents. Long story short, Dr. Eddy discovered that the monkey tissue used to create the polio vaccine had an inherent virus (SV40) capable of causing cancer. When she attempted to share her findings with contemporaries and her superiors, she was essentially fired from her job and censured. This was in 1960, after millions of children had been vaccinated with the Salk IPV (inactivated polio virus); meaning millions of kids carried the SV40 virus and may have passed the virus on to their children. And, although there is evidence that the SV40 (simian virus) may have been present in humans before the inception of the polio vaccine program, many scientists are not in agreement as to the extent of the polio vaccine's role in the increased incidence of the virus and the associated potential cancers. (12) In this example, the standards of some pharmaceutical companies and their leadership are suspect in that important medical information was withheld from the public for an extended period. The U.S. government supported the mandatory polio vaccine program even after the acknowledgment of the SV40 contamination. Independent researchers in France, Germany, Italy, and Japan have found evidence of the SV40 virus in brain cancers and bone cancers, and as a potential cofactor in mesothelioma (lung cancer). (13) In 1972, Dr. Eddy testified before Congress on the continued use of the (IPV) polio vaccine in question: "I guarantee you that over the next 20 years you will have epidemics of cancer unlike the world has ever seen." (14)

Vaccines were, for a time, a very lucrative product for the pharmaceutical companies to make and distribute with the backing of the AMA and the government-mandated vaccine program targeting school children. The limitations of the vaccine schedules become apparent as the program to vaccinate the children is essentially a one-time event in the respective child's life. As more diseases were eradicated from the tapestry of America, the manufacture of vaccine declined, and some medical watch dogs condemned big pharmaceuticals and the government for being "short-sighted" in the event of the sudden return of an extremely infectious disease.

The swine flu fiasco of 1976 was the beginning of extreme public scrutiny with respect to government-initiated vaccination programs intended to "protect" the public. Many will remember the vaccine actually killed some seniors (within hours of their receiving the shot) and numerous others were stricken with Guillain-Barre Syndrome, a disease that caused neurological damage, including paralysis. There was also heightened political controversy, as this was an election year. Some of the issues included the CDC (Centers for Disease Control) giving the vaccine maker the wrong strain of flu virus, quality control problems during the hasty production, and the Congress passing a quick bill to fund the plan intended to immunize every man, woman, and child in the U.S. In the fog of manufactured panic, there came the question of who would receive the most from the $136 million dollar plan. Remember Jonas Salk and his nemesis Albert Sabin? They were used as promotional tools to sell the plan to Congress and ultimately the American people. Of the 45 million people that were vaccinated, thankfully there were only fifty-three deaths. (15) Fast-forward to the year 2009 and we see history potentially repeating itself with H1N1.

Over the years, pharmacology has opened the frontier to phenomenal new product lines for the pharmaceutical companies. These include chemotherapy drugs to fight cancer and psychological drugs to fight depression, impotence drugs to encourage amour, and behavioral drugs to control children with ADHD, to name but a few. One possible motive for all the new drugs is that vaccines are not the money-generator they once were. The trusty United States government will always need vaccines for the armed forces troops, and as Government Issue, our troops represent a captive audience to test the latest in vaccine pharmacology. Some will recall the Gulf War syndrome and illnesses that plagued returning veterans of Desert Storm. At the time, it was indicated that biological agents and defective vaccines were the likely pathogens. The children of these veterans had an abnormally high incidence of birth defects; many of these abnormalities were distinctive in manifested affliction. We can rest assured that the remaining drug-makers would find the time and manufacturing capacity to produce any designer vaccines that could or would be specified for the benefit of the American populace.

Cancer has now become one of the most lucrative motivators for the drug companies. Cancer drugs such as Herceptin can cost as much as $4,000 per month, or $48,000 in one year for one patient; others, such as Avastin, can cost $10,000 a month or more, and that is some serious medicine! Drugs like Remicade, that treat rheumatoid arthritis, can cost over $20,000 for a year's treatment.

Just as one thing leads to another, we find the research scientists in pharmacology constantly bringing new drugs to market for medical and public consumption. The frustrations of trial and error lead researchers to find success in failure; this is and will be the case with the side effects of some questionable medical initiatives, like the polio vaccine previously examined.

A new vaccine that has the potential to eradicate, or at the very least attenuate, the human papillomavirus and potentially prevents cervical cancer (associated with sexual activity) is called Gardasil. This drug has the unique distinction of potentially stopping cervical cancer and illuminating the power of the medical monopoly to alter the moral fiber and ethos of the American culture.

Why is a drug of this nature targeted at girls as young as 9!? Girls younger than 17 should be strenuously discouraged from sexual activity until mature enough to handle the seriousness of an adult activity. Understanding the tremendous drives of the adolescent libido should not necessarily be an avenue of driving revenue for the promotion of a vaccine. One in four American girls ages 13 to 17 have been given at least one shot of Gardasil, and the Centers for Disease Control has added the vaccine to its routine childhood vaccine schedule, with 11 and 12-year-old girls being encouraged to receive the vaccine. (16)

Merck & Co., the creator of Gardasil, aggressively marketed the controversial vaccine to several medical groups, with the ultimate goal of gaining widespread support and endorsement of their product. Merck admitted to paying almost $200,000 to ACHA (American College Health Association) and $250,000 to SGO (Society of Gynecologic Oncologists) for what was classified as funding for education about the vaccine. (17) Since its 2006 FDA approval, the vaccine has been found responsible for 32 deaths and 12,400 major medical traumas through August 2009). (18) In the year 2008 alone, Merck had worldwide sales of $1.4 billion dollars for this single drug. The *Journal of the American Medical Association* has written about this latest medical advancement at length. With the endorsement of JAMA, the vaccine will be accepted and promoted worldwide as a weapon in the fight against cervical cancer. For this reason, it would be unpopular to suggest that a drug intended to fight cervical cancer could later be found to cause sterility and any number of other maladies after additional years of actual societal use and further analysis. Note: Gardasil for boys was FDA-approved on 10/16/2009.

Another controversial issue, that drug makers ultimately will be judged by, pertains to the additives in vaccines that have been associated with and vehemently suspected as the cause of autism in young children. The very nature of vaccine relevance is counterintuitive with what is known of the human immune system in the 21st century. To include metallic elements in a vaccine that are known to be deleterious to the human body suggests a nefarious intention.

Some of the major drug manufacturers chose a hard-line stance against the possibility of one of their principle vaccine ingredients, thimerosal, contributing to the increased incidences of autism and encephalopathy (brain damage) in babies that had received mandatory scheduled vaccinations. Extensive studies related to child vaccines indicate that cumulative high dosages of mercury (a component of thimerosal) can be a causal agent in the onset of autism. (19)

The controversy began to escalate with the ever-increasing early subjection of infants to mandatory vaccinations that were, in many cases, unwarranted. In many documented accounts, normal, healthy, happy babies were turned into zombies within hours of receiving certain vaccines that contained thimerosal and (in some instances) aluminum. (20) Aggressive campaigns and lobbying by the National Vaccine Information Center (NVIC) and others led to the FDA encouraging the vaccine manufacturers to stop using thimerosal (1999), especially in infant vaccines. (21) However, thimerosal was still found in "adult" vaccines (2001). Dioscorides (40-90 A.D.) would be proud of the advances in pharmacology, a science that the physician sought to perfect during his practice in the reign of Emperor Nero.

The large pharmaceutical companies, as previously mentioned, are an industry unto themselves. Like all capitalistic entities, profit is their principle motivator. Their power to shape public policy is an admonition for the citizens to be ever mindful of motive with respect to the questionable necessity of some vaccines. Let's briefly recap: No vaccine is 100 percent safe; no vaccine is 100 percent effective; some people have died from bad vaccine; in most cases, money is the principal motivation for the promotion of the vaccine. In addition:

1. "Vaccines cause immediate, sometimes drastic, adverse reactions.
2. Vaccines have unknown long-term adverse effects, which may include persisting autoimmune disease and nervous system damage.
3. Vaccine efficacy may decrease over time, making children susceptible to disease as adults, when complications are more common.
4. Many vaccines are questionably effective." (22)

The band of corporations that complement drug-makers most are, you guessed it, the original apothecaries. By the late 1950s, many school-aged children, members of the "baby-boom generation," were prescient in knowing that their huge demographic of humanity, born between 1946 and 1964, would grow old one day and need the latest in advanced medicine. As one of the roughly 78 million comprising the group, this writer does not want to paint an insidious back-drop to the idea of being born to supply illness for a small group of pharmacological oligarchs executing elaborate sanguinary expropriation of wealth. But this is very close to the reality when one peruses the balance sheets of the big three drug outlets that include Walgreen, CVS, (Consumer Value Stores) and Rite-Aid.

The economy of the United States is roughly 14 trillion dollars (2008), with the medical monopoly equating to nearly 17 percent of that, or 2.3 trillion dollars. A further inquiry finds that the big three drug stores combined account for at least 6 percent of the money expended on health in America, more than $125 billion in drug sales. Add in Wal-Mart drugs, and the figure easily eclipses $158 billion. (23)

These numbers do not tell the whole story, only a harbinger of what is to come. The huge group of "boomers" is rapidly aging and has become the principal reason why CVS and Walgreen are opening one new store each, every day. The actuaries know that the pool of new elderly has 7,200 people turning age 60 every day in America, for the next 15 years! This is truly a target rich and captive audience to be sure. This is the reason why Wal-Mart, has ventured into the drug market and has aggressively attempted to take market share from the predominant big three.

The rapacious competition between CVS and Walgreen speaks to the huge potential and real earnings from the aforementioned group that is destined to live, on average, longer than their parents before them. In most cases, these "boomers" have resources to pay for life-extending medicine, and that is well within the purview of the medical-monopoly. The medical-monopoly has computer model projections on the exponential increase in drug consumption by the targeted group, referencing all ranges of medical illness and associated medicines, especially those related to the elderly.

All Walgreen outlets are linked by computer, which allows convenient individual access across the country; CVS matches its competitor with similar ubiquity. With over 20,000 outlets (and growing) around the U.S., the big three pharmacies, and Wal-Mart, will eventually be more plentiful than McDonald's. The computer network(s) happens to provide an extremely rich data-base for government "oversight" or possible seizure and exploitation. Through the use of the "Patriot Act," the government is able to access any computer database for any reason, real or manufactured. The Constitution is eviscerated in the quest to find terrorists. Since many politicos have espoused the benefits of computerized medical records, the fact that all major drugstores already have considerable private citizen information available should not be taken lightly.

In fact, computerized records became a serious legal concern for CVS pharmacies in 2007 when the state of Texas sued CVS for violating the 2005 Identity Theft Enforcement and Protection Act. The drug supplier evidently dumped confidential patient information during the course of a business acquisition. (24) This same drug merchant has been involved in numerous health fraud and Medicare fraud scandals, agreeing in 1995 to pay $161 million in criminal and civil fines for paying kickbacks to doctors and submitting inaccurate billing charges to the government. (25)

Medicare fraud appears to be a fairly common venture in illegally acquiring taxpayer monies. The United States Medicare system is a federal program that provides health care for 45 million people that are over 65, blind, or disabled. With a budget that is approximately 450 billion dollars (2009), it is easy to comprehend the motivation, for multiple interests, to "tap" the system. As previously detailed, doctors will have a piece of the action; various medical suppliers (wheelchairs, scooters, medical accessories), deserve their share; and we must not forget the insurance gods. One particularly odious example of fraud deserves dishonorable mention. In Miami FL, FBI agents and federal auditors discovered elaborate sham contractors, rampant false claim fillings, and pseudo home health nurses supposedly administering insulin to non-existent patients. (26) Between 2005 and 2009, 700 people have been charged with fraudulently billing Medicare for more than $2 billion dollars in the Miami area alone.

We can extrapolate that similar fraud is being committed in other large metropolitan areas, especially where there is a high senior citizen populace. If we add in the estimated 500 billion dollars spent on purported unnecessary medical care, we begin to realize the extent of the corruption, illusion, and losing proposition that we call health-care; and what constituent parties use as a stage for wealth appropriation. Insurance deities round out most of the remainder of the 2.3 trillion previously enumerated; with an estimated $360 billion related to administrative costs or intentional waste by precept. Contrary to common belief, malpractice insurance does not constitute as much of the excesses as claimed by some pundits, no more than 1 to 2 percent. (27)

The inefficiencies of the federal government are well documented. And that is why it is futile (incomprehensible) to believe that a government-mandated, all-inclusive health care program could ever work with accountability or efficacy and is sustainable for any period of time. This is especially true with the resource network system currently in place. It is dubious to believe—in all honesty—that government officials sincerely want the system to be reformed, much less operate with efficiency. Remember, it was by congressional duplicity that an anti-trust exemption was put in place to protect the insurance companies and their system of lobbyists (bribery). Those in charge are able to use "leakage" as an off-the-books cash card that facilitates graft and other questionable activity outside of oversight.

At this point in the analysis, a much more sinister aspect of medicine has exposed one of its veiled facets, unable to completely disguise itself. Medical science, as arcane and abstruse as anything known to humanity, has provided a quasi-serendipity that could be classified as a scientific dictatorship.

Medicine has evolved to not only lengthen the lives of mere mortals, but also serve as a mechanism for population control. The philosophy, psychology, and utility of the medical arts, in execution and effect, are designed first and foremost to extend the lives of those in the aristocracy. As was clearly outlined in the history of AMA medicine, money is the ruling motive in medicine; this fact is exemplified by the perverse actions of the insurance companies, pharmaceutical companies, doctors, lawyers, and most importantly the government. As a control measure, the government knows that men and women treasure their one true prize, life itself. Carefully rationed and extraordinarily valued, health care is an inducement for the masses to act according to the dictates of the state.

More importantly the oligarchy, which is derived and controlled by members of the aristocracy, has perfected scientific dictatorship in a model that serves multiple purposes. These powers know that our society is predicated on as many people as possible reaching the stage of a productive (working) citizen so that citizen can pay taxes into the system and support the aristocracy. This is true for those who do not work but are essentially plutocrats and supreme beneficiaries of the system. The system must have a semblance of equilibrium, that being economic viability and controlled warfare. This allows the vast majority of masses (preferably young) to work and support the system, within production limits and a given life-span. As many grow old, and the birth and death rate of humanity remains in balance or fluctuates, the government will encourage or discourage life-sustaining measures. The over-arching principle is the preservation of the earth's resources specifically for the aristocracy.

The super-rich and their chosen associates have no worries about receiving the absolute finest state-of-the-art medical care because the aristocrats own, or control, all aspects of the system. As world populations grow beyond what is perceived or deemed sustainable, the government (plutocracy) will utilize passive-euthanasia, controlled pandemics, and warfare to obliterate those considered dead weight. This is evidenced time and again and as the most important resources begin to diminish, the scientific dictators will manipulate the system to their desired conclusion.

The idea of a scientific dictatorship is not new. In the early twentieth century, several advanced philosophers had extraordinary precognition in predicting the state of humanity in the future with respect to population growth, viable government, and the earth's resources. In 1932 Aldous Huxley wrote the novel *Brave New World* that envisioned a dystopian society chemically controlled (drugged) in all aspects of human behavior. (28) Although futuristic—for the times—and filled with artistic irony, the premise of the work is eerily cogent with respect to contemporary America—especially in light of a 2009 study that indicated the use of antidepressants in the U.S. had doubled from 1996 to 2005. (29) Add in "self-medicated" illicit drug users and Huxley's dystopia comes boldly into view, contributing to the system aforementioned.

Another Englishman and Nobel Prize laureate, Bertrand Russell, deserves a closer look. Russell (1872-1970), is famous for his mathematical genius and even more so for his contributions to twentieth-century philosophy, which was an amalgam of socialism and pacifism. A prolific writer and lecturer, he wrote the noteworthy book *The Impact of Science on Society*. Bertrand Russell was also either prescient or immensely influential because in this book he wrote: "Diet, injections, and injunctions will combine, from a very early age, to produce the sort of character and the sort of beliefs that the authorities consider desirable, and any serious criticism of the powers that be will become psychologically impossible. Even if all are miserable, all will believe themselves happy, because the government will tell them that they are so." In the same book, Russell goes on to speak of the probability of a "scientific oligarchy" and the inevitable totalitarian power it would ultimately yield to the state. (30)

These insights seem to explain, to some degree, why the Food and Drug Administration (FDA) is combined as one unit. There also remains the question raised earlier: why would a drug-maker include poisonous materials like mercury, aluminum, and formaldehyde in vaccines that are made for human protection? This could be rhetorical, but this writer is loath to know or believe beyond a reasonable doubt. Evidently, Bertrand Russell knew something…

The vaccine laws (injunctions) insist on giving a new-born baby a poisonous injection before the infant has drawn two breaths outside the womb. On the opposite extreme, an individual suffering with cancer may have to pay $10,000 dollars to receive life-sustaining drugs for a few more days of life or maybe a remission. Note: Few middle class families can afford the exorbitant cost of medicine in this example, much less the poor, and all concerned know this. The medical insurance companies can arbitrarily cancel coverage at the end of the term; and a pre-existing condition could be a death sentence. This is often the case even after the insured party has faithfully paid the premiums. The lawmakers are influenced—controlled—by legalized bribery known as lobbyists (remember AMPAC, PMA). But they insist they have genuine concern for their constituency and that the fault lies with tort reform, or hospitals, or suppliers, or the pharmaceutical industry, and they—are innocent. The doctors are still on the scene but they are insulated by their various front organizations, many having evolved from the original AMA.

The catalysts for many interrelated medical mysteries return to the AMA in an enigma that requires historic inquiry. The caduceus, a medical organization symbol that consists of a rod entwined by two snakes and capped by a pair of wings, originated from a Greco-Roman compilation. This symbol is emblematic of the esoteric fraternity that dominates medicine in all facets and with omnipresent consistency. Apparently the symbol was originally *The Staff of Asclepius*, the name of a famous physician from ancient Greece who practiced medicine around 1200 B.C. Through myth and legend he came to be deified as the Greek god of healing. After the Romans conquered Greece, they adopted the original staff with two snakes and added their own legend, so that Hermes (Greek) became known as Mercury (Roman). Mercury, the mythical messenger of the gods, had wings to fly and although there were several legends, the Roman imperative became the perennial favorite in the early days of the AMA. (31)

There are multiple associations with the caduceus, some negative, and these issues may have prompted the AMA to drop its use as the emblem of the organization in 1912 and adopt the strict use of the staff of Asclepius—that being the rod and two snakes only. The symbol with the wings remains prevalent in military and commercial operations and has its own group of ardent promoters. (Note its prevalent use by various news networks). Both symbols are representative of the Roman Empire including the attendant controversies related to the practice of snake worship, magic, mythology and the occult.

Buy Some Money

There are many individuals that will recall their first sentient experience with the unit of exchange known as money. You may have even been taught, from an early age, to understand what money is and what its intended uses can bring to your life and its purpose in a civilized society. Few will ever really know or endeavor to try and understand the true nature of money, and this is one life's unending tragedies. Civilization predicates all matters of existence on a whimsical commodity that has rarely been properly identified or explained, and is mysteriously cloaked in the manifested ideal that, to this point in time, only a few can truly possess to their desired extent. Economic utility appears remote and resources are, in effect, an abstract depending on your individual perspective or station in a given cultural society. With this in mind, we may find the true nature of money to be a source of liberation or a prison of incomparable horrors.

Throughout recorded history, we find that variables pertaining to wealth were indeed transient; and various indigenous people had their own sense of what constituted wealth, or what we call money today. Through the development of sciences, such as paleontology and anthropology, we know that there was a time when animal skins, beaver pelts, flint and other rocks, and of course food sustenance, were all used as exchangeable commodities serving as units of barter. As man advanced in intellectual refinement we note that the units of exchange evolved into the items of the most essential and those that were rare. In all accounts one overarching principle controls the essence of any unit of exchange, that being what humans choose to infuse their life force into, and this is what makes the object command a determined value. The locale and ethos of a given culture obviously have a tremendous influence; and that, too, is subject to the entropic counterinfluences of a given system and the worldwide system as a whole. "One man's trash is another man's treasure," or so the adage goes.

Because a unit of exchange, money, must be energized by the people that will demand it, the system that serves the people in a monetary capacity must be ascribable to all of humanity. This axiom speaks to <u>all</u> human origin, in that all that are assigned to this planet come into life (born) with no material possessions and will also leave (die) with none. Advanced societies may make laws that are designed to protect and or deny wealth to those outside of an avaricious construct intended to consolidate all of the earthly (people's) wealth in the hands of a small minority.

In this tactile world we are resigned to the realities of our limitations; that includes our illusion of creation. We are incapable of actually creating anything; we can only transform materials of this planet into more desirable and useful conveniences. An iron worker can make steel from iron-ore that came out of the ground (earth); and he can use energy to make the heat needed during the process that also came from the ground, whether it was coal, oil, or natural gas. Another entity can take that same steel and fashion the parts to make an automobile and other items of perceived value. The same fact applies to anything produced by man, excluding procreation. In coming to a complete understanding of this reality, what then is money as it relates to the limits of origin?

The answer is invariably bound by the life force that humanity suffuses in all possessions and claims as such. In the final analysis, money must be acknowledged as ***units of life energy***. Our life energy is equal to our limited time on this earth and is further personified in what we choose to value. (1) When we chose to trade our time, energy, and emotional commitment, we became transfused with the money that we sought in relation to the value we place on our lives. It is only from this perspective that we can more accurately equate what money truly is if we are obtaining the life granted to us and desired by individual identity.

It was the nobility of the Middle Ages that may have first identified the connection of life energy and the value of time. From the time of the Carolingian Dynasty and Charles Martel, there was a determined drive for the rise of the feudal system; special hereditary rights, privileges, and wealth were afforded to those of a certain blood-line. The system was further expanded by Charles the Great, better known as Charlemagne (742-814). This was after the fall of the Roman Empire, and feudalism ultimately became the dominant form of government after the Germanic invasions and the Franks' ascension to western European dominance. Feudalism, simply stated, established an economic system of and from the land,—an agrarian economy. The peasants (or vassals) were consumed in working the land so that a lord (King), who owned everything, could live off of the life energy of the vassals. Sure, the peasants had a place to live and some food to eat, but not much else. The vassals may even have been required to fight and die in the lord's conflicts; which speaks to the contemptuous nature of life energy being exploited for the questionable good of a single blood-line. This system was very beneficial to the kings and their families but exemplifies the inequity that many faced and one of the principle causes of numerous wars.

Centuries pass, and the Age of Enlightenment arrives with the knowledge that precious metals and other materials constitute real and portable wealth. (Obviously the empires of antiquity knew that gold and silver were rare and thus valuable, but they were unable to construct and exploit a system with any stability). This was not the case with England, France, and Spain; these boys and girls knew that what was rare, and encouraged for possession, would establish true power and wealth for all times. Most of you know the story of mercantilism and a country's quest to hoard gold and silver. This was controlled through trade by the monarchs, the ones with the blood-lines. During the reign of Queen Elizabeth I (1533-1603), an Englishman by the name of Thomas Gresham (1519-1579) came to her aid during a time of extreme financial distress (too many expensive wars). Gresham could be considered the first true economist and was instrumental in identifying the debasement of English currency and the monetary axiom attributed to Gresham, "bad money drives out the good." It was Gresham that counseled the Queen and identified problems with the gold currency; evidently King Henry VIII had reduced the gold content of English coins years before. The solid gold coins were leaving the country and the debased coins were left, ultimately weakening the English economy. (2) For this reason and those pertaining to the exchange rates of various currencies of other countries in Europe, Thomas Gresham proposed, received approval, and financed the construction of the first Royal Exchange of London, which opened in 1571. The Royal Exchange would ultimately become the financial center of Europe by 1603, and one of, if not the most powerful money centers on earth. The exchange burned to the ground twice over three centuries, being rebuilt on the same site larger and more ornate each time.

With the evolution of mercantilism, the goal of growing a respective country's economy became the impetus for developing new innovations in international trade, finance, and world power. Identifying gold, silver, and copper as principal commodities and thus, money, they became the undisputed units of wealth. These metals had developed a powerful identity as money throughout the world and were destined—especially gold—to become the standard of a country's financial power. As world populations grew and the demand for more and varied products increased, the limitations of heavy metals became an impediment to economic growth. Metals were heavy and, as a consequence, required overhead costs to store and move back and forth between countries. There was also the chance of pirates robbing a ship during an ocean voyage, or worse yet the ship being sunk with a massive amount of gold and/or silver commodities lost in the sea. Out of the needs and desires of merchants and respective governments, various entities sought new and enterprising ways to use "notes" as media of exchange to alleviate, to some degree, the inefficiencies of bulky, cumbersome precious metals.

Formal banking activities existed in medieval times with noteworthy groups such as the Knights Templar of the eleventh and twelfth centuries and the Medici of Florence, Italy in the fifteenth century. With the Royal Exchange of London as a backdrop and English financier William Paterson, the central bank of Great Britain became the first modern bank to be established and incorporated in 1694. The bank was controlled by the English government and was instrumental in development of the first system to facilitate payments between entities that may not have had existing accounts. It was also the first bank allowed to distribute non-interest-bearing bank notes.

By the eighteenth century, many banks had developed a system of collateral loans and the collection of interest, primarily from farmers and small business. In Frankfurt Germany one very aggressive banker named Mayer Amschel Bauer (1743-1812) sought to make major loans to governments, with the intention of growing a banking empire of monumental proportions. This business executive saw an opportunity with King George III (1738-1820), in helping him to combat some discontented Americans in a far-off colony of the Crown. Mayer Amschel arranged for 16,800 Hessian soldiers to be placed at the King's disposal (for a reasonable fee) and gained the King's favor. Some palace intrigue ensued and an unexpected death of a benefactor in 1785 placed Mayer Amschel in charge of the largest fortune in Europe at that time. (3) Amschel had executed his plan to perfection and with a fortuitous stroke of luck became the subtle power behind the throne of the English monarchy. This was established by financing the many conflicts (some covertly staged) of the era, including the French Revolution 1789-1799 and the subsequent English wars with France in the years 1793-1815.

With the prosperity that Mayer Amschel achieved, he began to advertise his commercial corporate identity under a distinctive logo, a large red shield that featured an eagle symbol. From this point forward he became known as Rothschild, which means red-shield. Mayer Amschel Rothschild was forward-thinking in his quest for riches and immortality. He had five sons and after he died his will gave strict instructions and left a billion franks to set up each one of his sons as bankers in strategic locations throughout Europe. Nathan, the third oldest, drew the London branch and became the most influential; little brother James, down in Paris, would defer to and act in concert with big brother—as did the other three—and manipulate the course of many wars and the fortunes of nations. (4) All of the sons of Mayer Amschel were well schooled in the insidious manipulation of financial loans, money, usury, and covert government control. There came a time when a nation succeeded or failed on the word of the Rothschild financial dynasty!

The American Revolution was, to some degree, influenced by Rothschild interference. If the new-found Republic was to be, then it should be encouraged to pay a tribute to the Crown from whence it came. And this was the beginning of the secret plan to enslave America by stealth and through human vice...

> *"Give me control over a nation's currency, and I care not who makes its laws."*
>
> Mayer Amschel Rothschild (1743-1812) (5)

Mr. Rothschild had a thorough understanding of human nature, identifying the desire for instant gratification and the willingness to surrender real wealth in a transaction, with an anticipation of greater wealth eventually in the future on not-yet-earned money. (6) The ensnaring nature of a bank exploiting usury invariably corrupts the lender and the borrower in a disparate symbiosis. Insatiable greed sets in for the banker and emotional distress eventually envelops the debtor.

These forces can be used to create "economic provinces" to the detriment of a sovereign nation. Some examples of this include banks making loans to both sides in an armed conflict (war); this ensures that those operating the banks will profit no matter who wins, and at the expense of many lives lost. The revelation is not in merely knowing this, but coming to the realization that the perpetration of such evil is practiced as an art form, without the slightest regard for the loss of life.

The American Revolutionary War ultimately became the nexus between the genesis of a great country, based on individual freedom, and the dark forces of a secret tyrannical cabal. Agents of the Crown and various sub-factions had vested interests in the development and growth (tax revenue) of the new colony known as America. King George III had the burden of overcoming the indifference among his people left from his grand-father, King George II, combined with the challenges of an evolving world theatre and the loss of control over a major colony. These factions included the likes of "The House of Rothschild" and would have to be considered one of his principal advisors. Amschel Mayer, through the financing of groups like the Freemasons, and conceivably Adam Weishaupt (1748-1830) and the Illuminati of Bavaria, would conceive of the possibilities of using such groups to infiltrate and subvert the government of the nascent country formerly owned by the Crown. (7)

This scenario is credible, owing to the fact that mid-way through the Revolutionary War (1780), many of the King's advisors conceded the probability of the colony winning the war and gaining a free and sovereign status. By creating the illusion of acceptance, and covertly controlling activity behind the scenes, the monarchy could continue its parasitic drain of wealth from a young and vital host, America. The vitality of America had been surmised and coveted by factions in the monarchy early on; this was evidenced by the ever-increasing taxes levied and the unreasonable long-distance laws decreed from an ocean away.

Long before the start of the Revolutionary War one of the colony's favorite sons, Benjamin Franklin (1706-1790), had sagaciously sought to diffuse the brewing hostility between the upstart colonists and mother England. Ben Franklin had made an occupational sojourn to England as a young man in 1724, living and learning amongst his European brethren for two years. At only 18 years of age, the experience undoubtedly instilled at least some measure of allegiance to Britain and evidently to the King as well. It was at about this time in England (1717) that the Freemasons made their resurgence in formal activity. The exploits of Ben Franklin are well chronicled and he indeed made major contributions to the formulation of the United States. The questions that will invariably recur speak to Mr. Franklin's Freemason associations and his espoused—tacit—affinity for the monarchy of the eighteenth century.

By 1748, Ben Franklin was a wealthy and established luminary, eventually becoming a powerful political dignitary for Pennsylvania. In 1754, as a delegate to the Colonial Congress in Albany, he espoused the plan for a colonial union with the hope of placating England; this was an attempt to end the French and Indian war and save face. On the surface this would appear to be adeptly diplomatic; and although the initiative failed ratification, Franklin always contended that it would have prevented the Revolutionary War. (8) A colonial union essentially meant remaining subservient to the British Crown, not exactly the freedom that so many had zealously pursued. On another extended trip to England in 1757, Ben Franklin remained in Britain for five years as chief representative of the colonies. It is well chronicled that Franklin spent time with many noteworthy Englishmen, befriending the likes of David Hume, Adam Smith, Joseph Priestley and others. It is also known that he became a Grand Master Mason in Paris. (9) With all of the secret components attributed to Freemasonry, is it possible that Benjamin Franklin had divided loyalties? Of the original signers of the Declaration of Independence, Franklin has the distinction of being both Master of a Masonic house in Paris and Grand Master in Pennsylvania. He is also one of only three Masons to sign both the Declaration of Independence and the ratification of the Constitution, along with fellow Pennsylvania members Robert Morris and James Wilson. He was also part of the coalition of John Adams and John Jay that were appointed to sign the Treaty of Paris for peace with Great Britain in 1783. Ben Franklin also had at least a minor role assisting Alexander Hamilton in setting up the department of Treasury, with Hamilton as the first Secretary of the Treasury in 1789. Of the eight Masons that signed the Constitution, seven went on to have highly successful careers, including George Washington, the first President of the United States.

The U.S. Federal Reserve notes in circulation throughout the world feature seven denominations of currency with Franklin as the top dignitary to grace the $100 bill. With the exception of Alexander Hamilton, on the $10 bill, all of the other bills feature presidents. This is compelling and speaks to the breadth of encomium conferred on Mr. Franklin. In attempting to determine the criteria used to justify Franklin as the "King" of the currency money, it would be logical to conclude that only those that lived or were born during a certain time frame, from the signing of the constitution, would be eligible for such honors. Using such logic would mean Ulysses S. Grant (1822-1885) $50 bill is the youngest to be so honored; as currency notes featuring McKinley, Cleveland, Madison,

Chase, and Wilson are no longer found in circulation. All of the current dignitaries, so honored, have arguably made major contributions to the early cohesive successes that have served the country to this point in time. There are multiple enigmas associated with our most revered Patriots and the money that we use (constitute) as wealth. George Washington (1732-1799), first U.S. president and considered by many to be the father of the United States, holds the distinction of projecting the existence of a hidden government through the many mysteries in plain view on the back side of the $1 bill.

The United States seal, with the eagle as one part and the all-seeing Eye as the other, represents the nature of those that operate through stealth and insidiously control the destiny of America. How ironic for the first president to be the featured keeper of deception. In circulating this money it is easy—for the American populace—to become desensitized and resigned to the fate that the secret rulers hold in store for America and the world.

George Washington became a Freemason at the age of 21 in Fredericksburg, Virginia. It is doubtful that Mr. Washington was completely oblivious to the questionable propriety of any organization that operates in secrecy. Some historians have stated that Washington was resigned to never return to England, much less be involved in any secret plots against his beloved America. (Note: A statue of George Washington stands majestically in Trafalgar Square in London, and George Washington was technically employed by the British Crown, as well as being a direct descendent of English immigrants). There is an apparent contradiction in the endorsement of a foreign power being allowed to control any aspect of another sovereign country or government while espousing freedom and claiming to be a patriot. Washington supported (ordered) concessions be given to the British in the controversial Jay's Treaty of 1794. Just like many politicians of today, someone made George "an offer that he could not refuse."

The back of the $1 Federal Reserve Note is indicative of the colossal hubris of the Illuminati and the Freemason organization. Contrary to many sanitized explanations, the Eagle is descendent of the Roman Empire and was the leading religious symbol of the Roman Legions for going in to battle. In fact the Eagle Standard was an ornate statue that was placed on a pole and marched ahead of the individual Legion as a sign and projection of Roman military power. (10) The Eagle Standard was such an integral part of Roman religion, lore, and ethos that, upon losing two of the

Eagles in the infamous Teutoburg Forest massacre (9 A.D.), the Romans searched for the statues and plotted bloody revenge for six years. Not only did the Roman army of Tiberius find the Eagle Standard (15 A.D.), they mercilessly killed all of the Germanic tribes that were even remotely involved with the Teutoburg massacre. The Eagle commanded power and also those that revered the mighty bird of prey.

A. M. Rothschild knew of the Roman history; this is why when he adopted the red shield as his emblem, it included an eagle with five arrows in its talons—symbolic of his five sons. (11) The modern adaptation on the Great Seal of the United States shows the Eagle with thirteen arrows and thirteen leaves with olives and thirteen stars. This was purported to represent the original thirteen states but wait; when the original document was signed, there were only twelve states officially as Rhode Island refused to sign. Only after the government was long in place (1789) and Rhode Island was threatened with the stigma and taxes of import duties did number "thirteen" officially sign a year later.

The thirteen arrows in the Eagle's talon represent the five Rothschild sons and the eight signers of the Constitution led by George Washington and Benjamin Franklin. The complete list consists of Anselm, Salomon, Nathan, Karl, and James Rothschild; Masonic signers include John Blair, David Brearley, Benjamin Franklin, Robert Morris, William Patterson, John Rutledge, George Washington, and James Wilson. Although the violent connotation associated with the arrow suggests malice, be advised that those individuals that cooperate receive the good talon and the olives!

The all-seeing Eye comes from the Freemason's Illuminati-derived policy of seeing all as the illumined ones and always being on top of the masses (the body of the pyramid). The eye, or all-seeing Eye of Osiris, is similar to the triangular emblem that has graced the stationery and magazine of the Scottish Rite of Freemasonry for decades. (12) The Roman numerals at the base of the pyramid indicating 1776 are purported to represent the Declaration of Independence and the founding of America; this date unfortunately shares a corresponding duality with the Illuminati, a secret society founded on May 1, 1776, by Adam Weishaupt. (13) The Latin writing and language of Rome, *Novus Ordo Seclorum* means The New Order of the Ages—or "New World Order."

Thomas Jefferson (1743-1826), third U.S. President and the primary author of the Declaration of Independence, was a man of intellect and contradiction. These contradictions are shrouded in his zealous conviction for the sovereign rights of a free and independent state. This and his contempt for debt-based money were two of the reasons for the vitriolic relationship that existed between Jefferson and Alexander Hamilton. It appears that the flamboyant Hamilton may have been influenced by members of the English banking cartel, and the vigilant Jefferson found out about it. He wrote an opinion that argued:

"If the American people ever allow private banks to control the issue of their currency, first by inflation and then by deflation, the banks and the corporations that will grow up around them, will deprive the people of all property until their children wake up homeless on the continent their fathers conquered." (14)

Ironically, this prognostication apparently came true in the year 2009. The crooked bankers (along with politicians) are able to loot the banks through "government decree" and charge the theft to the American taxpayer. Thomas Jefferson may have been the principal balance and anchor in the complex tandem of discipline and freedom representative of America.

Alexander Hamilton (1755-1804) holds the unique distinction of being appreciated far more in death than in life. He is the only dignitary honored in visage on U.S. currency but not eligible for the presidency; and yet the passage of time reveals that Mr. Hamilton left an indelible and endearing mark on the United States. His determination to have a central bank and paper currency did benefit the U.S. as did the federal collection of taxes to fund the operation of the government. His interpretation of the constitution, although deemed abrasive at the time, has come to be used as a standard with respect to interstate commerce and the balance of power between the states and federal government and the implied powers inherent in the constitution.

Vilified late in life as an adulterer (quite the ladies man), he was subsequently redeemed by the public when he fell to Aaron Burr's bullet in a senseless duel. With ten as the cardinal number, it is easy to understand why Hamilton would be so honored. On the surface, it could be construed that Hamilton favored the Crown and may have been influenced to use the style of bank finance that was endorsed by The House of Rothschild. (Hamilton was born a subject of the British Crown on the island of Nevis and was probably influenced by bank agents of the British Crown). More importantly the monetary policies instituted by Hamilton did benefit the country at a critical time. The premise of debt being the catalyst for the growth of money was embraced by Hamilton and an analysis, in hindsight, suggests it contributed to the steady growth of the United States. (15) This remains a factual statement even if the system has grown demonstrably out of control, as was predicted by Thomas Jefferson and revisited by Andrew Jackson.

Andrew Jackson (1767-1845) was the seventh president, the first true president of the people to come from humble origins. In many ways it could be said that the preservation of the Union began with Andrew Jackson. The controversies that ensued over the nullification crises in South Carolina beginning in 1828 set the stage for the challenges of state rights over the excesses of dictatorial federal government control. (16) Andrew Jackson was even-handed in his approach to compromise, owing to the fact he was cautiously against a national central bank and in favor of state-run banks. (17) Jackson was an adherent to the doctrines of Thomas Jefferson with respect to the centralized bank. Some of Jackson's concerns included: "exposure of the government to control by foreign interests, concentration of the nation's finances in a single institution, it served to concentrate more wealth in the hands of the rich, and it exercised too much control over members of Congress." (18) By 1833, Jackson had nearly eliminated the national debt, ultimately becoming the only president to ever totally balance the budget of the United States. The controversies surrounding Andrew Jackson are multi-faceted and this small overview is intended to speak primarily to his visage on the $20 bill, perhaps a reference to Jackson ending the twenty-year federal charter to the second national bank that he never came to trust. Some believe that banking interests (opposing Jackson) were behind the failed 1835 assassination attempt on his life by a crazed gunman named Richard Lawrence.

Abraham Lincoln (1809-1865), is perhaps the most revered of all the U.S. presidents to date, for what should be self-evident among the majority of Americans. Preserving the Union was but one dynamic in the presidency of Lincoln; teaching the American people why is the most profound aspect of a well-chronicled nexus in history. Lincoln was also able to discern the flaws of a poorly conceived and corrupt monetary policy. Just before his assassination and in his fifth year as Commander-in-Chief, President Lincoln offered these words of caution:

"As a result of the war, corporations have been enthroned and an era of corruption in high places will follow and the money power of the country will endeavor to prolong its reign by working on the prejudices of the people until wealth is aggregated in the hands of a few and the Republic is destroyed. I feel at this moment more anxiety for the safety of my country than ever before, even in the midst of war." (19)

The aforementioned President Grant will always be tied to the administration of President Lincoln. This is not intended to slight Mr. Grant, simply an analysis in the shadows of his military success. This comes with the realization that the aftermath of the American Civil War would ultimately challenge several presidents leading into the late nineteenth century.

By the 1870s the banking system of the United States was in constant turmoil; this included the problems associated with the end of the Civil War and a lack of solvent banks. With the vacillation between state-run banks and the ideology of a federally-controlled banking system a lack of reliable currency stymied markets and financial stability nationwide. The competition between gold and silver and the conflicts of redeeming specie (coin) money with paper money created suspension of payments and the associated hardships. These are the earliest examples of the debilitating effects of a poorly conceived and inadequately funded banking system that emanated from the northeastern part of the country without uniformity or conviction. (20)

The financial panics of 1873, 1893, and 1907 provided the linking motivations of the banking elite to establish a nationwide or "Federal" banking system. (21) One of the most important aspects of a national plan would be the ability to provide "elasticity" in operation, one which is able to supply money as needed and also contract the money supply in the objective of controlling inflation. You may recall that Thomas Jefferson condemned this type of bank money because of its inherently corrupting and damaging nature.

In 1908 President Theodore Roosevelt created the National Monetary Commission; this was a direct response to the financial panic of 1907. Senator Nelson Aldrich (1841-1915) (Senator of Rhode Island), became the "king pin" of the group of men that would formulate a financial system that would control all aspects of money (wealth) creation, distribution, and ultimately collection in the United States. Senator Aldrich aligned himself with the likes of industrialists J.P. Morgan, treasury official A. P. Andrews, Charles Norton of the First National Bank of New York, Paul Warburg (an associate of The House of Rothschild) and others in developing, in secret, a plan to control the money that was to come from the Federal Reserve System. (22) From the very beginning, the "Aldrich Plan" was met with justifiable abhorrence as it revealed the ultimate and intended concentration of wealth into the hands of the New York bankers. So wantonly egregious were the specifics of the bill sponsored by Aldrich and his cronies that Congressman Charles Lindberg, Senior, testified before Congress on 12-15-1911 about the inherent corruption of the plan:

"Our financial system is a false one and a huge burden on the people...I have alleged there is a money Trust. The Aldrich plan is a scheme plainly in the interest of the Trust...Why does the Money Trust press so hard for the Aldrich Plan now..." The Aldrich Plan is the Wall Street Plan. It is a broad challenge to the Government by the champion of the Money Trust. It means another panic, if necessary, to intimidate the people. Aldrich, paid by the Government to represent the people, proposes a plan for the trusts instead..." (23)

These words are very similar to some of the threats that were perpetrated by former Treasury Secretary, Henry Paulson, in September and October of 2008. Paulson met before multiple congressional committees in his quest to get the Troubled Asset Relief Program (TARP) bill pushed through Congress. In other words, the modus operandi of the privately held Federal Reserve Bank is the same, one-hundred years later. Henry Paulson was doing the bidding of his Wall Street and London superiors. "The former CEO of Goldman Sachs told Congress privately that if they rejected the bailout bill another great depression would ensue, that there would be a breakdown in law and order as well as food riots and civil unrest...that the situation would terrify the American people and lead to an even bigger problem." The fact that the entire purpose of the bailout was switched as soon as it was approved by Congress proves that Paulson's threat was nothing less than financial terrorism and a successful effort to blackmail Congress with hastily manufactured doomsday scenarios. (24) This was financial tyranny at its best and was used to further tighten the grip of the bankers' hands around the financial throats of the American people and "legally" steal more wealth.

This is the first lesson alluded by this chapter; if you are to "buy some money" you must be prepared to bribe your representatives (as Aldrich apparently was) and endorse the Wall Street mantra that "greed is good; greed is right, greed works." (25) The passage of the Federal Reserve Act on December 23, 1913 was the beginning of the end for the freedoms espoused by the United States. It appears that 1913 was a banner year all around for the money men. They also succeeded in getting the sixteenth amendment to the constitution signed into law on February 3, 1913 and in full effect on February 25. The ability to tax income "from whatever source derived" is beyond legitimacy with respect to the taking of a person's life energy!

The ability to create the units of exchange for a nation, out of thin air, and then tax what is inherent to a free man's being, borders on an insanity that totally eclipses megalomania. The grandiose notion of monarchical supremacy that originated and emanates from the British Crown is more relentless than death—and has the same connotation. The United States may have gained political freedom from Britain through the Revolutionary War, but financial freedom from the Crown posed a far greater challenge. In devising an insidious plan to retain possession of its "colony" the Crown decided to use techniques of deception rather than military force, with money and its attendant trappings as the ultimate method of control. It seems London, England cannot resist the notion of conquest and domination, and this hunger is steeped deeply into its DNA.

From the first century A.D., the Roman Empire relentlessly instigated warfare to subjugate the Celtic band of barbarians on the mysterious island of Britannia. Emperor Claudius I actually thought he had succeeded in 43 A.D., but peace in the new Roman province was not to last. The spirit, culture, and religious ethos (Druidism) of the Celtics ultimately wore down the overstretched Roman Empire. Hadrian's Wall, built in 126 A.D., would have to be considered an elaborate public works project and mostly symbolic. By the third century, the Empire had learned of the relentless nature of their subjects and guerilla warfare was a constant occupational hazard emanating from these "conquered" subjects of the Roman Empire. (26) As with many of the subjugated barbarians, the conquered learned from their oppressors; adapting and evolving to live free at all costs and, by force of will, becoming the hunter and not the prey...

Londinium, as it was named and founded by Rome, has gone through several metamorphic changes in two millennia. It was burned to the ground in 61 A.D. by intractable subjects of the Empire, and was rebuilt—on the same site—numerous times and with variations of the name that essentially became London. (27) Wars and several more burnings could not deter the people (culture) from rising from oppression, destruction and internecine conflicts to become an omnipresent power of incomparable resolve.

Through the many centuries England has become synonymous with conquest. "The character of the British Dominion is different from any of the great empires that have preceded it." (28) Britain's insatiable quest for domination and the world's riches is clearly evident in a startling historical record: for over two hundred years beginning with its insinuation into the French and Indian War in America in the 1750s, that eventually led to the American Revolutionary War, and then to the Napoleonic War, Turkish War, Opium War, Crimean War, American Civil War (England interfered behind the scenes), and ultimately two world wars up through the mid-twentieth century. England has the distinction of being involved in or at war with virtually every country on the planet at one time or another, at least thirty wars over the two-century period outlined. (29) These facts speak to the proclivity of avarice that is suffused throughout the country's entire realm of existence. The Opium War of 1839-40, between Britain and China, is a perfect example of Imperial Britain dictating to a sovereign nation how it would conduct business within its borders. Ultimately Britain collected vast amounts of money from drug trafficking (opium) and arranged a treaty to exploit Chinese Hong Kong for an extended period, making even more untold wealth. Throw in the pillage of African resources like diamonds and gold, and well, you get the picture. These examples pale in comparison to the banking industry of London that dominates the world financial kingdom. The City of London is the world's largest financial center, with New York City listed in subordinate second place. (30)

New York is subservient to London by virtue of the interlocking alliances that were established dating back to Alexander Hamilton. The tentacles grew stronger in 1908 with Teddy Roosevelt and his men; they included Paul Warburg, J.P. Morgan, Jacob Schiff, Bernard Baruch, John D. Rockefeller and Senator Nelson Aldrich. (31) All of these men had ties to the New York bank that ultimately became the Federal Reserve Bank of New York, the king pin of all twelve reserve banks. They all met in secret on Jekyll Island, Georgia to finalize their plan, culminating with Congressional approval. With the new law in place (1913), the Bank of England became the principle stock holder in the banking affairs of the United States and this included tax collection and distribution. This writer often wondered why New York was titled "The Empire State," and now the answer is clear for all to see.

The Federal Reserve Bank is the mechanism that the aristocracy uses to steal the life energy of the people. The Federal Reserve creates debt instruments that are presented to the people as money. Calling it money is an outright lie. The money that we use is <u>units of debt</u>, and virtually everything that is purchased comes through the eternal weight of usury. In devising such a system, the rapacious bankers are assured of everything technically belonging to them. Here is how it works. When you apply for a loan the banks issues a "note" that is simply an accounting entry. The terms of the loan may be for a five-percent interest charge. The bank then issues the amount of the loan to the borrower with the terms of the total to be repaid, including the interest (usury). The problem is that only the loan amount is actually issued, which means the interest amount remains outstanding, even after the loan is paid off. What this means is that what is purchased is, by technicality, never actually paid for. For example: a loan amount $20,000 dollars at a six-percent interest rate. The total amount of interest payments may be as much as $2,800 (or more) depending on terms and the speed of repayment. But when the loan is repaid the bank will remove the original $20,000 from circulation but the interest, which was never "officially" created, remains on the bank's account book as outstanding. This money is ultimately removed from the system and creates a money shortage so that the people (economy) must constantly borrow to have money in the system. Now you know why credit card companies encourage credit usage and the intention of holding high balances at 26% interest or more to keep money circulating in an inherently corrupt system. (Note the increasing number of payday loan outlets).

"The only thing that we here in America may use for money under our present system is debt. Every dollar must be borrowed into existence for the exchange of wealth to be facilitated within our nation. Since every dollar must be borrowed into existence, the natural corollary to this is that every dollar has interest attached to it for every moment that dollar exists. Once you understand compound interest, it is easy to see how this will lead to massive amounts of debt. And not just the so-called national debt, but the accumulated debt of every man, woman, child and business in America as, everyone desperately attempts to borrow enough credit to keep themselves and their family afloat." (32) Here is the second lesson of how you must buy some money to exist in an inimical system.

The system compels an individual to essentially pay with something that does not really exist, beyond the implicit belief. The United State has been on and off the gold standard many times over two centuries. President Nixon removed the United States from the gold standard for the last time in 1971. Without any true substance backing the fiat money created by the Federal Reserve, there is no real money to truly speak of. The illusion of wealth is in the illusory of usury.

Let's look at a larger transaction with a large contractor. One billion dollars is borrowed at eight percent interest. The same rules apply only this time the $80,000,000 of outstanding debt (interest) remains on the books and will eventually be retired from the system. In this example it was a government agency that took out the loan and the outstanding account balance becomes part of the "deficit." Now multiply this by thousands of times and include millions of John Q. Publics and you get a sense for the incomparable wealth that is "created" out of nothing and paid for by the public for the benefit of the bankers.

The Federal Reserve can alter the rules of the game during the game if it so desires. If the "fed" determines it needs to raise interest rates, one net effect is the altering of the perceived value of a given collateral, estimated future earnings, and the cost of buying your money! It becomes even more insidious when the house that was purchased for $100,000 and with interest payments you paid back $250,000 is only worth $75,000 when adjusted for inflation and depreciation that the fed manipulated over the course of 30 years.

A bond, Treasury bill, or note—it makes no difference; they are all instruments of debt. This means that no matter whom or what entity holds it—save the banker—the wealth produced will eventually (through various mechanisms) come back to the Federal Reserve Bank. "The underlying methodology of this system allows for no other possible result except that all wealth becomes concentrated in a very few hands." (33) Let's not forget those "mechanisms" also known as taxes. The tax laws that were enacted in conjunction with the Federal Reserve Act serve to keep the illusion alive and well by servicing the "debt" and keeping the masses in a hybrid gilded-cage type of bondage. Property tax is one example. You paid taxes on a major purchase (boat or car) at the time of purchase and then, for the life of ownership, you pay property tax year after year on something that you have supposedly already paid for! The real irony is, if you and millions of others had not purchased anything, there would not be any money in the system to pay taxes on anything, with the system that is currently in place.

In the year 2000, it was estimated that Americans were paying upwards of sixty-five percent (65%) of their income on cumulative taxes. Some studies indicate that percentage to be closer to 80% in 2009. (34) This system is only sustainable by the ever-increasing amounts and decreasing value of what we use as money. The current real deficit (2011) is in the realm of $55 trillion dollars. To service this debt billions have to be paid in interest every month (18 billion per month in 2011), with little (no) chance of paying it off and, as previously explained, must be perpetuated for money to be available. This is the pinnacle of insanity. Our children will soon have to learn the mathematics of quadrillion and eventually quintillion respectively, as trillions of dollars will be needed to service the debt in future monthly interest payments.

Recall the understanding of what constitutes real money with respect to our lives. The units of exchange that we use are packets of time. As the bankers manipulate interest, taxes, and access to needed materials, the unit of money (time) becomes devalued for the common man as the rich bankers or aristocracy take the time expropriated from the masses to enrich and better enjoy their lives. "Inflation is simply the process through which the time (the life force) of the people is appropriated by the privileged few for their own personal benefit and gain. The most important fact is, firstly, that the bankers must keep this process secret for fear that the people will awaken to what is going on"… (35) As the taxes and inflation go out of control and less people can afford the system, the bankers (Crown) repossess land, houses, and businesses and eventually own everything; which was the ultimate goal all along. This is emblematic of the seal on the first president's dollar bill; the All Seeing Eye represents the aristocracy holding most of the wealth while sitting on top of the lowly masses.

The distinguished historian and scholar Carroll Quigley wrote extensively about the money men and how their plans for world domination would be secretly carried out in his masterpiece, *Tragedy & Hope*. Professor Quigley documented the interlocking alliances and the historical plans of the money men, dating back hundreds of years. (36) A bank of England governor named Reginald McKenna was quoted in a famous speech stating: "I am afraid the ordinary citizen will not like to be told that the banks can, and do, create money….And they who control the credit of the nation direct the policy of Governments and hold in the hollow of their hands the destiny of the people." (37)

John Maynard Keynes, the celebrated British economist, was a proponent of government spending during times of economic recession. Keynesian monetary philosophy, used in modern economies, is generally considered a principle component of modern economic theory. Mr. Keynes wrote a treatise in 1919 on the consequences of inflation: "By a continuing process of inflation, governments can confiscate, secretly and unobserved, an important part of the wealth of their citizens. By this method, they not only confiscate, but they confiscate *arbitrarily*; and, while the process impoverishes many, it actually enriches some…" (38)

The sons and adherents of Keynesian monetary philosophy have served their father well. By perfecting the combined forces of usury and taxes, the bankers are able to target industries, neighborhoods, and islands of economic influence to rape and pillage at will. A perfect example of this returns us to the former Treasury Secretary, Henry Paulson. As earlier delineated, Mr. Paulson used threats to encourage Congress to pass a massive bail-out bill to re-capitalize banks that had made some ill-advised loans, credit default swaps, derivatives and malfeasance. After receiving the money, Mr. Paulson changed the criteria and the purpose of the over $1 trillion dollar tax-payer-funded bailout package. When asked where the money would be used, Mr. Paulson became evasive and refused to give a clear answer. Senator Jim Inhofe of Oklahoma was one of the few representatives of the people to have the courage to press for answers and called for the "blank check" to Mr. Paulson to be cancelled. (39)

The Treasury is indeed an invincible force for the status-quo. Representative Ron Paul has been calling for an audit of the Federal Reserve since 1983, and he has been systematically blocked by members of both political parties for over 25 years. (40) The private ownership of the Federal Reserve allows the bank to operate with impunity under the guise of being classified as a "Federal" entity. This is part of the deception that perpetuates the rape of America and its people. Remember what Thomas Jefferson and Andrew Jackson stated in their condemnation of the foreign money powers and what was discovered by Carroll Quigley. There can be little doubt that the problems America faces are by design and, in many cases, are the actions of nefarious individuals that have committed Treason against the United States. The accomplices of the countries pretending to be U.S. allies are in fact our enemies and the vilest form of bloodsucker known to man. The bankers and their affiliates have joined forces to make laws through the purchase of elected officials.

This climate of theft from the taxpayer is personified by notable crooks such as Bernard Madoff. The convicted swindler Madoff is but a choir boy in relation to the "big boys" that operate behind the scenes and out of sight. Madoff was able to perpetrate the biggest "known" financial deception in Wall Street history. The most interesting aspect of the crime is that the SEC or Securities and Exchange Commission was warned about Madoff and his questionable financial dealings <u>six times over a sixteen-year period</u>, and did nothing. (41) Here we have one of the finest examples of the government either unable or unwilling to enforce the laws within their purview. This speaks to either ineptitude or internal corruption, maybe both. Bernard Madoff, with the full force of a lobby network, may have used some of the $150 billion dollars to buy substantial persuasion in "legalizing" his scheme. Ultimately, the U.S. taxpayer will suffer and be forced to pay for this debacle and others such as Marc Dreier, another convicted crook that used deception and pretense to get away with over $380 million dollars. (42)

With Wall Street bankers as the gate keepers, perennial and increasingly audacious legalized thefts (extortion model) will remain the norm. In our electronic age, financiers such as Goldman Sachs (Henry Paulson's old firm) have perfected the science of "high frequency trading." By utilizing special high-speed computers built specifically for electronic trading—that include advanced stock market trading algorithms—these traders are able buy and sell huge blocks of stock in mere milliseconds. In some cases stocks are bought and sold within the time frame of one-second or less! (43) Those companies with such capabilities have a distinct advantage over the average trader and consequently make money regardless of how the overall financial market is performing. The implications of these high-speed computers reveal the ability for the operators of such a system to not only out-speed everyone but, in effect, subtly influence the markets in certain sectors. Senator Charles Schumer of New York has called for a ban on "flash orders" and has threatened to write legislation to eliminate the unfair advantage that belongs to the largest insiders on Wall Street. "This kind of unfair access seriously compromises the integrity of our markets and creates a two-tiered system where a privileged group of insiders receives preferential treatment, depriving others of a fair price for their transactions…" (44) Good luck to you, Senator….

Further examination of the irrepressible greed in the financial industry sheds light on the evolution of capitalism in the United States and the rest of the world. In the clarity of objectivity, we find that members of the middle-classes contribute to the tidal wave of desire and, although far removed from the phenomenal wealth of the Wall Street bankers, deserve some of the blame. The middle-class contributes to the drive for more of the aggregate wealth through the insatiable appetite for cheap goods from big box retailers like Wal-Mart. There is a reason why Wal-Mart is the largest retailer in the world; simply stated the demands of consumers encourage, to some degree, the drive to live the highest standard of life at the lowest cost. Noted economist and author, Robert Reich, succinctly explains this in *Supercapitalism*. (45)

With keen insights, Professor Reich makes the case that all consumers contribute to the motivations that drive the captains of the capitalist theatre to find new and enterprising methods to give the masses what is demanded. Case in point, the managers of huge pension funds and 401k retirement accounts are under intense pressure to earn maximum return for all investors and this creates pressures throughout the system. When huge pools of pension money are involved, which means John & Jane Doe, members of the middle class encourage (demand) the highest yields on their accounts. This allows them to be able to purchase more low-cost goods to maximize their lives. (46)

The common man, various large-block stock holders, and even the manufacturers all want maximum returns; which includes the fund manager and his attendant avarice. This brings us to the third and final notice on the purchase of your money, with the knowledge that the patronage of stores like Target, Wal-Mart, Sam's Club and other big box retailers recycle life energy (money) to the middle-class through technology and the tacit approval of capitalistic exploitation. Be advised that this is but one facet of the overriding issues of too much wealth in too few hands. This is also one of the negative side effects of technological advances when consolidated in the hands of those that can perpetuate the corruption of the leaders in our democracy—a democracy that was intended to serve all of its citizens. (47)

The Roman Empire instituted taxes to support and grow the civilization it envisioned from a composite of far-reaching visionaries, some from Greece and others so enchanted. In a controlled sphere of influence discipline is relatively manageable, even in an era of antiquity devoid of high technology. As the Empire grew and far-flung provinces became more difficult to occupy and totally supervise, communication and oversight broke down. Decisive and true visionary leadership is required in each location throughout an extended kingdom for there to be any measure of sustained progress. Fair and equitable taxation serve a purpose; excesses motivated by graft, bribery, and greed will eventually destroy an Empire, no matter how large or powerful. This is historically relevant when we analyze the issues that were prevalent in fourth-century Roman chronicles. The tax burdens in the mid-century contributed to peasants starving to death. (48) By 380 A.D. history indicates that taxes became so oppressive that tax riots began to increase in frequency, even with the penalty of death. In one case it was precipitated by what was described as a 'super tax' for a questionable state program. (49)

The spurious claims of the needed tax increases in the United States are a reflection of the problems (created and real) that befell the late Roman Empire. The United States is indeed a descendent of Rome and like father like son; the lessons of Empire are realized after it is too late. Incessant wars, disregard for the collective, and the self-ordained rights of the Kings and Queens invariably enable the crippling cells of carcinogenetic destruction from within. As venality becomes accepted and expected, this feeds the cancer with fresh supplies of blood and growth is assured to sustain the next act in a life-altering drama that few will escape.

All roads may have led to Rome, and perhaps that is a metaphor for what the United States could or should not be. As the young America adopted many aspects of ancient Roman society such as a similar government structure, a strong dominant military, a system of laws intended to support a civilized culture, and property rights speaks to how much we are like Rome and, through the passage of time, different as well. You need only look in your own wallet at the blue or gold American Express credit card that features in visage the Roman soldier standing guard over one source of your money.

Only nuance will separate father and son in the analysis that will invariably be made by the civilization that is to follow. Hopefully, whatever remains will temper the next culture to avoid demoralizing the true nature of money; which is essentially the life energy that we infuse in all aspects of our existence. This energy cannot rightfully be constrained in the hands of a few but should be shared in the totality of what binds us all.

BLOOD FOR OIL

Oil and water: they cannot mix. This is an axiom to rival most earthly mysteries; for you see they both provide our world with a unique paradox. One element is essential to all life and the other provides the desires of life. Both are intrinsically related through a third substance we call carbon. As carbon-based life, we should be able to coexist with another carbon inherent in the petroleum we exploit. Like the two hands on the human body, one is dominant, but do not discount the other, for as is widely known, it would be extremely difficult without one or the other. After having lived with petroleum it would be extremely challenging to live without it.

This is the central doctrine of United States energy policy and a national security policy imperative. Like the life-blood flowing through our veins so, too, must oil flow throughout the entire spectrum of civilization now known to man. In our world we must drink from the oil-well as if it were the elixir of life, so very much like a drink of water. Only through variations of assimilation do we dare confuse the two, and for this reason we must pay an extraordinarily high price to quench our thirst. The era of oil, as our principle energy source, has reached a pivotal point in history, one that will define our civilization's continued existence. (1)
Prescient oracles and the foremost scientific minds on the subject have spoken of the impending catastrophe for some forty years. The Hubbert curve predicting the zenith or "peak oil" is now upon us. Marion King Hubbert (1903-1989), accurately predicted the peak of oil production in the United States (1970), and that same formula has been used to predict peak oil production for the entire world. (2) With the United States consuming 25 percent of the world's petroleum, the geopolitical and pure

economics of this precarious situation will become increasingly more life-altering in the foreseeable future. With all of the alarms, why has there not been a more aggressive plan to neutralize the impending disaster? The sad fact is that the world has trapped itself in a four-dimensional corner with the discovery and adoption of oil as the world's foremost energy source.

After World War II, it became extremely apparent how much energy was concentrated in a barrel of oil. The United States contributed over six billion barrels of oil to the Allied war victory and consequently greatly depleted its reserves. (3) The war taught military strategists and industrialists many profound truths about the power and versatility of oil; as it was a lack of oil that contributed to the demise of Adolph Hitler and the Third Reich. The lessons of war and established geopolitics led to the United States forging an alliance with Saudi Arabia—the country that possesses 25 percent of the world's known oil reserves. In addition, the combined aggregate of neighboring countries such as Kuwait, UAE, Qatar, Iraq and Iran accounted for roughly 50 percent of known reserves at that time. American firms such as Standard Oil had established contracts with Saudi Arabia to develop oil production as early as 1933. (4) By the end of the war, initiatives begun by President Franklin Roosevelt were continued by President Harry Truman. The Truman Doctrine became the definitive policy for protecting the Saudi (and Iranian) oil fields from an advancing Russian takeover. (5)

The implied protection afforded the royal family of Saudi Arabia was through an explicit promise from President Roosevelt at a meeting with then-King Ibn Saud on February 14, 1945. (6) This was the continuation of an agreement that had evolved over the previous century between Britain and neighboring Kuwait. (7) Britain had been dependent on Middle Eastern oil for several decades and had also imported up to 50 percent of its oil from the United States before and during WWII. (8) Britain was also one of the first countries to establish oil contracts with Iran, dating from 1901. This is the principal reason why Great Britain had originally been the protector and beneficiary of the oil fields in the Middle East for many years. The aftermath of WWII and Iranian political unrest contributed to multi-faceted conflicts, principally over oil but also over several local factions contending for political identity and national control. These were some of the issues linking the United States to the Middle East, the world's foremost possessor of the black-gold that would feed U.S. dependence and mandate the continuous protection of the region for access to the valuable petroleum.

The duty of world-police-force now fell upon the United States, a responsibility that was to grow far beyond what was originally intended. By the late 1950s, President Eisenhower had established further geopolitical ties with the region, including monetary aid and the latest weapons for enhanced protection of the Saudi royal family. (9) American interventions in the region included involvement with Israel and its incipient statehood (1948) and incendiary wars along with the continuing theological conflict and disputed lands. The U.S. protection afforded Israel would come to be a serious source of tension in the region and, as is widely known, threatened the flow of oil in 1973. The United States involvement in the region would become increasingly more pronounced with each successive president. President James Earl (Jimmy) Carter followed the Nixon doctrine with the expanded Carter doctrine that would signal to the world that the United States was prepared to protect Persian Gulf oil—with American blood if needed. (10)

Beginning with President Franklin Roosevelt and leading to the Truman, Eisenhower, Nixon, and ultimately the Carter Doctrines, United States Middle East foreign policy, and especially energy policy, has evolved into the foremost excuse for controlled warfare and the inexorable military-industrial complex. By signing an unspoken Faustian contract for access to and the protection of a finite resource, the United States is ultimately committed to trading American blood for Arabian oil.

The Presidencies of father and son Bush forty-one and Bush forty-three, each had their own doctrines to adorn their respective presidential libraries. George H.W. Bush developed a special nemesis in Saddam Hussein, a tyrant that had been placed in power by the United States in one of the other "custom-made" presidential oil doctrines in the late twentieth century. George H.W. Bush initiated war against Iraq ostensibly to combat tyrannical aggression; however, a closer analysis suggests oil rights for Great Britain contributed to the decision. As previously delineated, a long-standing treaty and special oil contract had existed between Kuwait and England for years; this would have been one of the motives for Prime Minister Margaret Thatcher's vociferous opposition to any Iraqi aggression. (11) By using her influence with NATO ally George H. W. Bush, United States intervention was assured and oil shipments were ultimately restored. There was also the simmering and underlying antipathy for Saddam Hussein. President Bush took serious exception to Saddam Hussein and his intractable defiance of previously established boundaries. (12)

Saddam Hussein was given a bloody nose, sent to his room for detention, and consigned to think about his transgression. The exercise was intended to be a lesson for any would-be oil tyrants; honor the international oil agreements in effect or suffer the consequences. The Persian Gulf War of 1991 was just the beginning of an advanced U.S. energy policy to continue the distribution of Middle East oil on the international markets without restriction. The previous presidential oil doctrines were mere primers in comparison to the Bush-Cheney doctrine that was to come with President George "W" Bush in 2001. (13) The NEPDG or National Energy Policy Development Group was inaugurated by "W" in the first ninety-days of his administration. Although the president spoke to the issue of increased oil dependence from unstable Middle Eastern countries, he was less than candid on his plans for addressing the quandary.

No need to worry, Vice-President Richard B. (Dick) Cheney was anxious to help guide the newly established NEPDG team and inaugurate an auspicious start. You see, Mr. Cheney was the former CEO of the Halliburton Company, an oil-field services company that was deeply entrenched in all aspects of world oil production. Dick Cheney was part of a network of powerful and influential officials related to energy companies all over the globe. (14) Mr. Cheney had served during the presidency of Richard M. Nixon and was involved in the Nixon doctrine and most of the subsequent presidential doctrines. Dick Cheney, a former congressman, has held prominent positions in multiple presidential administrations; he is a natural insider. President Bush could, in effect, set auto-pilot and focus on matters more interesting in his new role as Commander-in-Chief.

Vice-President Cheney developed some of his extensive oil influences while his party was out of power, during the Clinton administration. Although employed in commercial capitalism, political aspirations, along with inclinations toward American hegemony, were nurtured and collaborated with other like-minded Republican warmongers that included Donald Rumsfeld and Paul Wolfowitz. (15) Imperious domination is part and parcel in United States foreign policy. This is exemplified in Washington D.C. through political think-tanks such as the Council on Foreign Relations (CFR). All political heavy-weights are members of the CFR and Cheney has been a prominent member of over 25 years. (16) The list of industrialists and prominent politicians contributes to the labyrinth of interconnected energy conglomerates and lawmakers that insure money and power are consolidated among the chosen few. Energy drives almost every aspect of our modern civilization and those that have a complete understanding of this reality literally rule the world.

There are many paths to hegemony in the name of petroleum and all that it affords an imperious power. Some of the world's great political scientists (prevalent in the CFR) have made careers out of political, and in particular geopolitical, United States imperatives. Many have aggressively sought to create quasi-governments within what is accepted to be the true and sovereign government under the U.S. constitution. Politics and money invariably conspire to perpetuate money and power through political and foreign policy initiatives. One such group has its genesis in the CFR and through the aforementioned interlocking ties contrived a plan to create the group known as the Trilateral Commission. This group was formed to act as a liaison and linkage for the oligarchs in the three identified regions, the Americas, Europe, and Asia, hence the triad. (17) The Trilateral Commission received zealous support from President Jimmy Carter and his highly touted new National Security Advisor Zbigniew Brzezinski. (18) Originally founded in 1973 by David Rockefeller, the new organization was served by Mr. Brzezinski with incisive fervor, even authoring a notable book on the obsolescence of national sovereignty. (19)

In succeeding years, Dick Cheney came to be a ranking member in The Trilateral Commission, thus further aligning himself with plutocrats in every corner of the world. (20) With this understanding, it stands to reason that the philosophy of "geostrategic imperatives" would be one of the foremost initiatives espoused and supported by the inner circle of the Trilateral Commission. In his book *The Grand Chessboard*, Zbigniew Brzezinski challenges the United States to "prosecute an integrated, comprehensive, and long-term geostrategy for all of Eurasia....America is now Eurasia's arbiter, with no major Eurasian issue soluble without America's participation or contrary to America's interests." (21)

With these pronouncements, understanding the origins of presidential oil doctrines is crucial in comprehending the continuous and increasingly contentious United States presence in the Middle East. The group of countries that will forever be a "global zone of percolating violence" include the usual suspects—Afghanistan, India, Iran, Iraq, Israel, Pakistan, Saudi Arabia, Turkey and the small satellites around the Caspian Sea that include Azerbaijan and Georgia. There are 23 countries in all that make up the specified zone; they each have their own special problems, and all are linked in some way to energy. (22) Energy being the operative term, which now includes natural gas distribution piped to various Eurasian buyers and the conversion of liquefied natural gas (LNG) shipped to various countries on freighters similar to oil tankers.

The countries that rely on imported energy are generally assumed to be cogs in a machine that are integral parts of global commerce. With the United States being the largest integrator of the world's commercial exploits, the U.S. has responsibilities that have evolved to insure that the "world-machine" operates unimpeded—by anyone. This is but one of the reasons for the advanced presidential oil directives instituted by George W. Bush. After the terrorists' attacks of September 11, 2001, a profound reality slapped the U.S. in the face: factions in the countries that we have imported oil from and provided military protection to (Saudi Arabia), wanted to hurt us. (As is widely known, fifteen of the nineteen 9-11 hijackers were from Saudi Arabia.) The attack included our old friend Saddam Hussein, even if from a remote perspective. The 9-11 attacks seriously impacted commerce on multiple levels, with almost all dependent on oil. The airlines did not fly for a period, affecting the industry and stockholders. Even after some semblance of normalcy was restored, there was an uneasiness that further curtailed business and the bottom line. This was totally unacceptable in a global economy.

The Bush Administration's Doctrine of Preemption was part of the National Security Strategy or NSS issued in September of 2002. This was the document that gave the United States carte-blanche in defending U.S. interests from even a remote threat of terrorism, including the disruption of oil production and distribution. (23) The erudition and semantics of the document are nothing less than geopolitical genius with respect to insuring that petroleum flows around the world, uninterrupted by any would-be terrorists. Essentially the document is constructed to include the act of withholding or destroying oil resources, as technically terrorism and would be considered an act of war. Moreover, the preemptive oil doctrine allows for any perceived threats to be swiftly and unilaterally addressed after sufficient verification through intelligence agencies or a blatant provocation from anyone deemed unsavory. The arena known as "the zone," previously delineated, holds the distinction of being at the top of the preemption list. Not good for terrorists such as the late Saddam Hussein.

In the first Gulf War of 1991, Mr. Hussein, in an act of desperation, had his military dump oil from tankers at a Sea Island terminal located in the Persian Gulf. This action was designed to thwart the potential landing of U.S. Marines. The oil spill was estimated to be in the range of 42 to 400 million gallons. A percentage of the oil evaporated, approximately one million barrels were recovered and 2 to 3 million barrels washed ashore in Saudi Arabia. The oil slick measured 40 by 100 miles at one point during the assessment and is considered the worst intentional oil spill in history. (24) In a serious act of sabotage, Hussein's men also set fire to a reported 700 oil wells in Kuwait, destroying an estimated 6 million barrels of oil per day and seriously damaging the Kuwait landscape, air quality, and economic life. (25) The fires were started in retribution, to punish Kuwait for overproducing oil and lowering the market price for petroleum. Saddam Hussein had effectively wasted a valuable finite resource in an attempt to win a war from an untenable position. This was a very serious mistake as far as U.S. and coalition forces were concerned.

Who knows what evil lurks in the mind of a terrorist and what twisted logic they may employ? Suffice it to say, the attack by terrorists on 9-11, the worst ever perpetrated on American soil, changed the world in a multitude of ways. They include but are not limited to travel, commerce, surveillance, immigration, financial transactions, and the evolution of warfare. This is where the melding of the NEPDG and the Bush doctrine of preemption, serve the interests of all in need of the life blood we know as oil. It also provides the geopolitical legalese to extirpate terrorists wherever they may arise. In the popular and often heralded words of President George W. Bush, "I want him dead or alive." (26) Obviously dead is more expedient and the terrorists did kill innocent American citizens in cold blood, so an eye for an eye+ must be fair. With guilt and policy firmly established, Saddam Hussein's death warrant was signed. Osama Bin Laden would come to serve his purpose on the periphery, but Saddam Hussein had pissed-off Poppa Bush and wasted American blood, both red and black-gold.

In hindsight the Bush administration's decision to fight a second Iraq war, instead of the terrorist haven in Afghanistan, was the equivalent of killing three birds with one stone. The tyrant Saddam Hussein and his sadistic sons were eliminated. This allowed the installation (support) of a regime more accommodating to U.S. petroleum imperatives. And the neighboring countries in the "zone" were given a front-row seat to behold American military power and geostrategic resolve. Iran, although insistent in being ever recalcitrant, will eventually have to bend to the coalition of countries that is led by the world enforcer—the United States of America. The brilliance of the Saddam Hussein epitaph is that he suffered the ignominy of a trial and the shadows of a gallows noose before embracing a most horrible death. The power of the spectacle resonated among the condemning party and those that were of captive witness.

Osama Bin Laden, after eluding capture and taunting the United

States for nearly 10 years, was killed in Pakistan by U.S. forces on May 2, 2011. His culpability in the New York, 9-11-01 terrorists' attacks is well known and American justice would not be denied. (27) In every drama there must be an antagonist and a protagonist. Osama Bin Laden worked exceptionally well because he contributed to a narrative that originated in his home, his culture, and in his deoxyribonucleic acid. Recall the explicit arrangement established with the Saudi royal family and President Roosevelt; the Bin Laden family has close familial ties to the same family. This same family has established extensive contracts with the United States Department of Defense (DOD) through the use of Iridium satellites owned by the Saudi Bin Laden Group. (28) These satellites, originally developed by Motorola, provide satellite telephone coverage across the globe. The communications network was purchased by the Saudi Bin Laden Group (SBG) in 1999. In addition, SBG is engaged in multiple DOD contracts that include high-frequency and magnetic energy field experiments using the Iridium satellites and other high-technology equipment. (29) SBG also owns the principal construction company of Saudi Arabia and was involved in the building of the U.S. military bases in Saudi Arabia, including Khobar towers. Saudi Arabia possesses 25 percent of the world's known conventional oil reserves. (30) The diplomatic relationship between the United States and Saudi Arabia has been firmly established and nurtured for over 80 years. It is based on the aforementioned geostrategic imperative and will never be even remotely challenged—by anyone! (31)

The phenomenal wealth that petroleum generates cannot be overestimated. The Halliburton Company received an initial $7 billion in tax-payer dollars in no-bid contracts to support government war operations in Iraq. (32) You may recall Halliburton is Dick Cheney's old company; in 2004, Mr. Cheney was the largest individual stockholder in the company, with holdings worth a purported $45.5 million dollars. (33) Between 2004 and 2008, Halliburton stock options rose an astounding 3,281% and prompted U.S. Senate inquiries. (34) Moreover, Halliburton received additional no-bid contracts for work in Louisiana after the hurricane Katrina catastrophe. These contracts were pushed through by the Bush-Cheney Administration, and estimates indicate Halliburton has received over $20 billion dollars for work in Iraq and the Katrina disaster. (35) It should be acknowledged that areas damaged by hurricane Katrina happened to be home to some of the principal regional oil refineries supplying petroleum products to the United States.

Petroleum development directly parallels the invention of the internal combustion engine. A case could be made for oil being the principal catalyst for the rapid technological advancement realized during the twentieth century. The various types of internal combustion engines (ICEs) that include the Otto-cycle, diesel, rotary, and gas turbine all use varying grades of refined petroleum. Most of these engine types are prevalent in transportation and contribute to a formidable economic effect throughout the world. The age of the automobile became the preeminent showcase for the use and evolution of the internal combustion engine, and consequently industrial capitalism, for most of the twentieth century. Through petroleum use, the automobiles came to constructively consume prodigious amounts of steel, copper, aluminum, rubber, glass, and various other materials that propelled the greatest industrial and economic growth in the history of man. (36)

Transportation, of every type, returns to petroleum development and the advance of civilization. Petroleum was especially beneficial for aircraft operations, since lightweight materials, including fuel weight, are significant for the efficiency of flight. "High energy content per unit weight of gasoline is more important for airplanes than for cars." (37) High grade aviation fuel that is derived from oil is but one example of the power of hydrocarbon energy. Petroleum has the inimitable quality of diversity in its interchangeability through the perfect composition of carbon and hydrogen molecules. Oil allows for the conversion of light and medium vapor gases and light, medium, and heavy liquid fuels. This is why oil is so highly coveted. The versatility of hydrocarbon fuels cannot be exaggerated; a barrel of oil is capable of yielding 18 different products, all highly utilized throughout civilization. (38) Oil also provides derivatives for the petrochemical industry, contributing to humanity through pharmaceuticals, medical implants, fertilizers, and oil-based polymers. (39) In fact, almost every conceivable plastic and rubber creation, including computers, plastic containers, sports equipment, automotive tires and clothing, has its origins linked to petroleum. (40)

The many virtues of petroleum have conspired to make its use indispensable. This was acceptable for the advancement of civilization and sadly, only for a limited time. Such is the nature of a finite resource, especially one with such unmatched power. Oil is not perfect. It takes a lot of former carbon-based life and elements to be pocketed, pressed, and cooked in living metamorphic rock for a long time for oil to be created. (41) Some scientists have postulated that oil is inorganic in nature and has its own unique genesis from the original formation of the planet earth. Both theories work for the good of humanity in current reality.

The ability to accurately find major reservoirs of oil and extract the product is a challenging, expensive and dangerous undertaking. The search for oil is an exercise in geological intricacy, precision and patience; it can be hugely rewarding and also financially crippling with dry holes, inaccurate seismic readings, or simply a well of insufficient pay-back. (42) Though there may be success at discovery, the challenge of extraction remains with a myriad of variables to be conquered. Many people imagine oil in underground lakes, easily pumped or under pressure for controlled extraction. The reality is oil eventually has to be pulled through solid rock, akin to sucking a viscous liquid through thousands of filters and up through a long straw. (43) There has to be some porosity or open structure in the containing rock formation for oil to find a path to the zone pickup point. The depth of oil origins and oil-well extraction points varies widely, with some wells producing oil at 500 feet. However, many of the larger reservoirs are in the 8,000 to 13,000 feet depths. (44) <u>Offshore-based oil wells are obviously more challenging, with potential oil spills and loss of accompanying natural gas pockets.</u> Storms, along with ocean-related dynamics, challenge oil producers to install a special drill template and foundation pile cemented in place—all in water potentially thousands of feet deep. (Note: this hazard was painfully realized in the devastating Deepwater Horizon Gulf oil spill that happened on April 20, 2010 and lasted for over three months). (45)

Oil producers are prepared to go to extraordinary lengths in the quest for the black-gold that drives the world economy in a precarious state of inexorable dependence. The vociferous cries of scientists and other sagacious minds are beginning to be heard. (46) But this alarm may have been acknowledged too late for remedial paradigms to be fully contemplated and incorporated in a salient geostrategy for civilization as a whole. The problem is of multiple complexities by virtue of the hierarchical monolithic concentrations of power that evolved throughout the twentieth century, with all being driven by the preeminence of oil. "Big oil and big business have gone together." (47)

What started out as a monopoly at the turn of the twentieth century, and was ultimately broken up, could not be constrained by any measure. John D. Rockefeller established Standard Oil through a rapacious capitalist model that ultimately became <u>the</u> model for the robber barons of the era. And although the monopoly was divided up through government anti-trust legislation in 1911, Rockefeller devised methods to circumvent the law, and make oil the dominant energy source in the United States. (48)

Oil is produced, marketed, and distributed—all by the same people. This means that the tankers that move the oil and the refineries that formulate the various fuels for the transportation industry are all owned, in most cases, by the same big companies. The fuel distributors and your favorite fuel outlet have an infrastructure of store-fronts, tanks, pumps, licensing agreements, and the blessing of the state controller to dominate the industry to the exclusion of all others. That is why small mom and pop outlets have gone the way of the dinosaur. Through exclusive contracts and agreements with all of the united banks, the petroleum men offer credit cards for the purchase of their fuel, further increasing their bottom line and reinforcing the use, method and system of fueling, with oil, the great country known as the United States. The CEOs of the big oil companies have the life-or-death assignment of maintaining energy domination at all costs. The billions of dollars invested in their infrastructure must be perpetuated until the last possible barrel of oil has been exploited, or the new system aligns with their continued profitability. (49) This attitude, philosophy, and avarice is comforted by the "live today and die tomorrow" doctrine that most purveyors of oil evidently live by. Leave the problem for the next generation and, by the way, our automobile manufacturers and jet engine builders have some of the same vested interests.

Oil doctrines of yesteryear have sustained the use of the system extant, based on the realization that all those internal combustion engines have many years of life left, and the need for the continuous projection of a dominant power. Plutocrats will eventually call for the dramatic curtailment of access to petroleum. One manifestation of this happened during the summer of 2008 when the price of a gallon of gas reached a record nation-wide average of $4.12 per gallon for regular unleaded. (50) In some states like California and Hawaii, prices exceeded $4.60 per gallon. (51) Some pundits have called for gasoline to be taxed to equal an astounding $6.00 per gallon—the ideology being the monetarily enforced conservation of the resource. (52) This logic has limited effectiveness in the United States by virtue of how much the American economy depends on millions of vehicles warming the highways and byways on the way to Grandma's; or the grocery store; or the theatre; or the football game; or the mall; or to dinner or, most likely, to work some of the time. And, for all those suburbanites, that is a really big deal. Because of our inherent dependence on essentially everything that oil provides a dramatic curtailment would be the equivalent of suicide for American life as it is known. Without a truly comprehensive and strategic plan that does not disrupt the social and economic fabric of the United States, dramatic and potentially devastating shock waves will be felt throughout all of civilization.

During the spring and summer of 2008, the escalation in gas prices sent convulsions throughout every city and locale in the United States. Dramatic and measurable fuel price resistance was felt. Exorbitant percentages of household budgets were constrained by fuel costs. These budget impairments resonated through the economic world and eventually affected everyone. Ultimately, capitalistic red ink led to the dreaded layoff, and many dominoes fell thereafter. Government agencies that monitor American economic activity came to the realization that the average American consumer, in 2008, had a limit in so far as how much expendable income could be allocated to gasoline.

This was the first harbinger of what will happen when peak oil shortages become chronic and progressively worse. Sadly, there will come a time when $7.00 per gallon will be a bargain. Much of this is owing to the fact that the U.S. and the world have been irresponsible in not aggressively promoting new fuel technologies. The time lag for adoption and acceptance of a new transportation fuel system is the primary threat that could lead to a premature destruction of our society as we know it. Much of the uncertainty relates directly to increased consumption of oil worldwide; countries such as China and India will place more pressure on the remaining oil that is in declining availability. Will wars be fought for the remaining oil? The potential reality has already been manifested in Iraq, to name but one example.

An intemperate irony must be acknowledged: In attempting to stabilize and ensure the flow of oil through world petroleum markets, the U.S. military consumes a sizeable amount of the finite resource that it is attempting to protect! A supersonic jet fighter consumes prodigious amounts of fuel, so much so that we have flying gas stations to accommodate mach-speed flight. Add military tanks, personnel carriers and assorted support vehicles, all relying on oil, and you get the picture. Various estimates indicate that 5 to 6 billion barrels of oil are consumed annually by the worlds' military. (53) This ideology hastens diminishing returns; and although some jobs are created and economic effect infused in society, the military-industrial complex effectively wastes vast amounts of energy. The world currently consumes 27 billion barrels of oil annually. The U. S. consumes 7.1 billion alone.) (54) If the military were to cut consumption by one half, we could extend the transition period while developing the new fuels.

Not the best of contingencies, as the world is past the point of contemplation or complacency. The combustion of oil becomes increasingly insane because of its inherent qualities and uses for more wide-ranging and beneficial needs for humanity (such as medicines). Estimates of between 900 billion to 1.3 trillion barrels of conventional oil remain (2010). Even if these estimates are low or high by 100 billion barrels, it would be the equivalent of between 33 and 48 years at the current rate of consumption. Gasoline rationing and automobile manufacturer mandates—small-displacement ICEs and hybrid gas-electric vehicles—could extend the remaining oil reserves. (55) (Transportation consumes 65 percent of the total oil used in the United States.) Again, the economy will influence to a large extent any and all remedial solutions. The issue of climate change, related to fossil fuels, is a subject unto itself, with the increasingly specious evidence of civilization-influenced climatology contributing to political and social divergence. Unless dramatic advances in alternative forms of energy are developed--including renewable energy—the United States and the world will have to adapt and accept climate change as a part of the vicissitudes of existence on this planet. (56)

PEAK OIL VERSUS PEAK GRAIN

Civilization is predicated on and exists through the consumption of energy. The types of energy that have sustained various cultures have consisted of two universally powerful necessities, those being food and a unifying force such as religion. The food supply is self-explanatory and immutable; every human must eat. With an ideal or the spiritual, the culture is subject to various factors including the strength of the dominant character representative in the core of origin. From out of a mythical story come two brothers born of sorcery, left for dead, resurrected and nursed by a she-wolf. Romulus, the dominant twin, killed his brother Remus in an allegory similar to that of Cain and Abel. It is from this life and death struggle that the city of Rome began, and with the act of its namesake and his brother's blood in the very mortar of the founding bricks. This beginning ironically would serve as a model for conquest for most of the formative years of the early Roman Empire.

Energy exists in many forms; however, few civilizations have ever been able to fully recognize the true nature and value of energy as it relates, in totality, to the limits of the planet and a given reality. In archaeological study, the Roman Empire serves as one of the foremost subjects for its complexity in multiple fields related to agrarian, confiscatory, and nationalistic themes that are associated with civilizations of antiquity. Roman imperatives contributed to the inherent drives that were evidently an irrepressible characteristic of the people and culture. This assessment is based on the irrefutable history: Rome dominated the known and acknowledged world for nearly ten centuries–a millennium. These innate personal drives may have been constituted by the perennial mythology of its progenitor (Romulus) and the continuous demand for blood, from both indigenous citizens of Rome and those that dared to oppose its destiny. Roman pride and resolve in predestination should be acknowledged as one aspect of the drive (energy) that justified Roman imperialism. "Remember, Roman, that it is yours to lead other people. It is your special gift."—Virgil, *The Aeneid*. (57)

Collective nationalism can be extremely powerful (note the initial unified nationalistic pride of the U.S. during times of war). This is the normal inclination in a society and even more so in a complex society that ultimately evolves into a state. (58) Rome, for a time, had high ideals that were identified as a code of virtue (*virtus*), in comparison to the barbarians. (59) In the empire's earlier years, foreigners were allowed to "ascend" to the lofty heights of Roman citizenship, generally after having been subjugated. To dominate vast numbers of conquered people requires discipline and endless supplies of energy, something that most emperors may have never fully contemplated. Conjecture speaks to where the hubris and imperious nature may have emanated, but the unrelenting thirst for conquest was far more than a necessity. The Roman culture ultimately set out to mold the world into an idealistic Republic polity; a quest that could be compared to trying to obtain the speed of light—with conventional physics. Fear, a small society that had outgrown its original environs and needed to grow with its circumstance, or perhaps divine provenance, the question(s) still intrigue scholars of history.

Most of the energy employed by Rome at the height of its dominion was supplied by the built-up inertia from multiple and highly successful military conquests. By 146 B.C. Macedonia had been seized and the third and final Punic war was ended with the destruction of Carthage, Rome's avowed nemesis for over 120 years. The treasuries of Rome overflowed with the booty of the conquered former kingdoms, now mere provinces of the Roman Empire. Hegemony eventually extended over Gaul (modern-day France and Germany) and with Gaul came wealth from gold, minerals, slave labor, and lumber from plentiful forests. (60) The aforementioned conquests were the crowning achievements of the immortal triumvirs, Gnaeus Pompeius Magnus "Pompey the Great" (106-48 B.C.); Marcus Licinius Crassus (115-53 B.C.); and the incomparable Gaius Julius Caesar (100-44 B.C.) the man more than any other responsible for Roman greatness.

Although his reign was short-lived, Julius Caesar left an indelible legacy and endemic influence on Rome. An analysis reveals Julius Caesar was shrewd in understanding the basics of human nature and apparently knew how to appeal to the people of his time. He was also fearless, standing up to pirates that kidnapped him at the age of sixteen. Held for ransom, Julius Caesar dared the pirates to fight him, and when the pirates' demand for his ransom amount seemed low to young Julius, he demanded—dictated to the pirates to increase the ransom amount. (61) And, the pirates complied. After receiving payment, the pirates released Julius, and he went on to finish his business on the island of Rhodes. The House of Caesar ultimately hunted down all the pirates and had them killed by crucifixion. Upon completion of an extensive education and military training, he became a highly effective soldier and leader on the battlefield. His charismatic appeal among his men motivated them to fight seemingly untenable battles, and win. This ultimately established powerful military alliances that would serve him all the way to the Rubicon.

Julius Caesar would become the archetype for the Caesars that were to follow. And although he lost sight of total reality, with respect to human foibles, (jealousy, fear, personal ambition, etc) he was smart enough to teach his young nephew, Octavius, (later Octavian) a few lessons that would serve him and the empire, for an epochal period. We all know what happened to Julius Caesar in March, 44 B.C., and we can only wonder what might have been. The love for J.C. became painfully evident when his assassination initiated a civil war in the Roman kingdom that was not easily extinguished. Octavian was not about to let his uncle's death be in vain. He aligned himself with some military friends of Julius (such as Mark Antony) from his previous historic conquests and the Rubicon River. This was the beginning of the Second Triumvirate and after 15 years of hacking and stabbing, with many assassinations, nephew Octavian became Augustus, first emperor of the Roman Empire (27 BC). One of the lessons that never failed Augustus was his humility with respect to title, emperor and not king. This is perhaps, among other things, why his reign lasted over 43 years; few emperors came close in duration or success. (Notable theologians imply that Augustus' reign, during the incarnation of Christ, was not a coincidence.)

The wealth that had been accumulating in the Roman treasury during a very lucrative confiscatory growth period was put to good use by Augustus. Corruption and greed continued but was attenuated by the steady hand of the emperor during the last stages of Rome's Golden Age. The emperor distributed coins to his subjects and even suspended tax collection for a period. Augustus was smart enough to curtail the advancement of territorial conquest for a while, which led to relative peace in the kingdom. Without fresh infusions of booty, and with no real industries to speak of, eventually greed and increased populations—which generally tend to happen during the good times—will erode the largest treasury and nominal food production. Once the energy source runs low, travails from multiple sources are sure to follow.

The plebians, various tribes, barbarians both indigenous and interlopers were all in need of energy; not to mention vast military legions. The provinces on the empire's periphery may have had a bad harvest in some years. Combine these issues with the fact that food shipments in 10 A.D. were very expensive over land, and that's without the problems of graft, brigands, and general depravity. Many of the "suburbanites" moved closer to Rome to have access to free wheat and other essentials. The middle of the third century (234-284 AD) would have to be considered the beginning of the end for the great Roman Empire. (62) The reforms of Emperor Diocletian (245-313) delayed the decline for a period and provided Constantine elementals for a Christian platform; however, the final acts were in play by the time of Emperor Constantine's death in 337. Compromised peasant farming, the over-farming of some farm lands, decreasing tax revenues, and conquered people coming to feed on the Roman dole—all contributed to depleted vitality in the Empire. There were other problems, like plague and excessive leadership changes (emperors murdered). The economy was stagnant or negative in growth, the expense of the military was unsustainable, especially with the reliance on expensive barbarian mercenaries. There came a time when lands were sold just to make payroll for the remaining lands and paid mercenaries that protected their own interests first and maybe the remaining empire second.

The Roman Empire faced a decline in excess energy but the outsiders had next to none. The established polity and the energy associated with it became an irresistible attraction for many thousands of hungry barbarians. By failing to anticipate the hunger of many and not being farsighted in planning for empire, Roman leadership failed to institute economic growth strategies like large agricultural farming and a deliberate—sustainable—system of food distribution. The notion of "imperial overstretch" contributed to the demise of Rome and the policy has serious implications for America: "the idea that one's security needs, military obligations, and globalist desires increasingly outstrip the resources available to satisfy them." (63) The laws of gravity and inertia will compel a huge boulder to continue rolling downhill for a long ways; so too will centuries of conquest perpetuate an empire, even as it begins to implode upon itself. The energy that Rome accumulated ultimately came to attract relentless barbarians of every ilk. These same barbarians adopted some of the tactics employed by Rome, and all were driven by a hunger of one form or another....

The United States has created a similar parallel by its insatiable oil consumption. Our neighbor to the south, Mexico, exports approximately 16 percent of the oil imported by the United States and has supplied voluminous oil for many years. (64) This tremendous amount of energy contributes to U.S. productivity and economic vitality. The Mexican illegal immigrants are very similar to the barbarians that invaded Rome—hungry for energy, riches, and a better life. Either through stealth or outright lawlessness, the illegal alien has come to consume energy reservoirs that are beginning to deplete the United States. The perplexing question is why a country like Mexico, with many natural resources (such as energy), cannot establish a vibrant and successful economy for its own people. Could it be rampant corruption or perhaps an unwritten agreement between the respective governments? The United States imports oil and the illegal immigrants follow the energy—fascinating.... Many people have wondered why U.S. immigration policy is not enforced; now you know why, it's the oil. The U. S. does not want to pass immigration laws that seem aimed at Mexicans because of the risk of offending our oil-producing neighbors to the south. The situation has begun to take a toll on places like California, with budget deficits that have to be attributed to illegal immigration in some measure.

In fact, the budget deficit that California incurred in 2009 is monetarily proportionate to the costs associated with illegal immigration. (65) Some of the parameters measured include illegal workers paid in cash, escaping tax collection; approximately 29 percent of illegal aliens being on welfare; illegal aliens having more children—placing added pressure on the medical system and the public school system with the additional costs being manifested in special provisions for multi-lingual education, and the issue of crime. (66) The huge shortfall in budget funding has caused some analysts to speculate that California could become the first failed state. (67) (An important component is the fact that California is considered to be the 8th largest economy in the world.) The governor of California has vowed to press for federal financial aid, with threats to cut state welfare programs if his requests are not granted. (68) With this probability, the U.S. federal government would be obligated to supply monetary aid, which would be a harbinger of the further decline of the United States. Because of the future of oil (energy), the situation is eerily similar to what befell the late Roman Empire.

The billions of dollars that the United States sends in oil deficit wealth per month to other countries could be allocated, to some degree, to develop new energy infrastructures. At one billion dollars per day, a mere 5 percent of this money would contribute $1.5 billion a month or nearly $20 billion a year for renewable energy research and the related support systems. If we include some of the military waste, the United States could be that much closer to a new dynamic and independent energy economy. The World Trade Center attacks on September 11, 2001, were a manifestation of Americans paying for U.S. oil policy with the blood of its citizens. We can trade sovereignty for oil; we have traded economic instability for oil; and if we fail to seriously confront the futility of consuming a finite resource, we will continue to trade blood for oil.

Special Note: *This treatise is not intended to disparage or condemn any particular race, nationality or culture. The problems identified with illegal immigration are for the purpose of contemplative analysis and understanding, with the expressed intent of learning from the mistakes of previous empires. The United States was founded and established, as it is, by numerous immigrants. And with checks and balances that are sustainable, the U.S. can continue to embrace immigrants and contribute to a more inclusive world.*

Sun Touch

Awash in the embrace of solar rays, nothing else compares in any measure. You need not be a sun worshipper to appreciate the warmth of its benevolence. Throughout recorded history we can attest to the relevance of the sun and how it could be the subject of deification for the early cultures and societies of antiquity. Time and destiny have revealed topical secrets of our nearest star and yet many remain unclear in its power to enable the existence of life on this planet. Our star, as far as what is known, is truly inimitable in its complex balance of nuclear fusion and perfect relative orientation in our solar system. Any closer and our planet would burn to a crisp, only slightly farther away and life would be frozen; much like Mars, the last of the true terrestrial planets in our very special group. An astronomical unit (AU), roughly 93 million miles, seems so vast in distance but in reality a mere walk in the park with respect to the galaxy. To exalt the Sun is to pay homage to its life-sustaining force and the principal source of the earth's energy, both direct and that which has been stored.

The Sun is directly responsible for the chemical photosynthesis of plants, which establishes the foundation of the food chain. Plants grow, providing food for animals of all types, and this supplies man with various food sources as well. The plants also absorb carbon dioxide and produce oxygen—something humans desperately need to live. Sure, this may seem overtly facile, but in light of the cap and trade proponents, fundamental refreshers are warranted. (1) These plants and a lot of dead dinosaurs were combined in a complex metamorphosis to create carbon-based energy known as coal, oil and natural gas. Geological chemistry and an abundance of heat and terrestrial good fortune conspired to endow this planet with multiple sources of energy, all directly related to the sun. The elementary burning of wood from the trees of vast forests is a source of stored solar energy.

We return to our star in the harnessing of atomic energy, and although controlled nuclear fusion on earth remains in its infancy, the relative association speaks to the inherent realities of the elemental component parts in this solar system. The thermonuclear fusion process that occurs in the core of the sun is related to the complexity of the very life that it supports. A truly cosmic scientific marvel whereby massive stores of heat and light are produced with supreme efficiency in a controlled proton-proton chain conversion of hydrogen to helium—in just the right balance without exploding—is truly phenomenal. (2) Although many stars are constructed in similar fashion, some can easily grow too large and therefore become unbalanced and explode into supernova. Our star will eventually become a red giant, in a complex death ritual not scheduled for another five billion years or so. (3) If our star had developed as a small-scale example, there would not have been sufficient heat for the planet earth to evolve and develop life as we know it.

On balance with some prevailing ideologies, it is easy to understand why some people would believe the earth to be the center of the universe; with all other potential life forms quite envious of our fantastic fortune. As our only point of reference, this planet naturally has to be the best for all we know. The knowledge of how our star is composed primarily of hydrogen, and the earth strangely has little of this element in pure form, suggests an intelligent design whereby the earth has alternatives that include uranium and the potential to duplicate the sun's energy, at least on a small scale. The finite resources the earth was endowed with help establish civilization and the intellectual concomitance associated with growth and advancement of sentient beings. Much of the solar energy reaching the earth began its journey from 170,000 to 200,000 years ago. In a strange irony, the energy created in the sun today could fall on an earth devoid of people in 2000 centuries… Not much more than a catnap for a star with a 10-billion-year life span. (4)

A billion years is a very long time, far longer than any human records. This writer has considerable difficulty imagining a million years… And yet, through the consumption of the sun's energy, both active and passive, kinetic and stored, we as a race of people have endeavored to comprehend these vast units of time. What has yet to be truly acknowledged is that in attempting to learn, understand, or exploit our earthly fortune, we have become lost in individual desire. For either personal acclaim or financial gain, too many scientists, politicians and megalomaniacs actually believe they have the power to control the earth. Sadly, this is senseless folly, akin to functional insanity within the construct of a devolving civilization. For man to seriously postulate that humans can actually change the cyclic nature of the planet, its axioms and mysteries, is in effect "foolishness, chasing the wind." (5)

The sun and earth existed long before man. The earth has existed and will exist without man; however, man cannot exist without the earth. Human beings are dependent on the earth, and to be clear, the earth is not dependent on human beings! In billions of years the earth has seen change and wonders far beyond human comprehension. Yes, we developed and possess intellect that has revealed some insights, but they pale in comparison to the complete story. And here is one of the foremost axioms for man; what has been bestowed upon man, earth, this solar system, is not within man's control. The best that the human race can expect to experience is based solely on the random complexity of a universe that created billions of suns out of cosmic dust and the microcosm of which is exemplified in the continuous entropy of one world among billions of others. As a race of earthly inhabitants, we would be wise to fully embrace the lessons and power afforded us by the sun. Knowing, in some measure, how the sun creates its energy is the first clue. The hydrogen that powers our star is distinctive and remotely differentiated from what the planet earth inherited; there is a message in this reality.

The basic carbon cycle identifies a natural earth system with respect to the elements that complement planet earth. We have known for years that the vast oceans dissolve most of the earth's atmospheric carbon dioxide and through this system redistribute this life ingredient through respiration, photosynthesis, combustion, death and decay. This is one of the controlling mechanisms for life on this planet, or simply stated, the nature of our earthly existence. As cultures mature into society and civilization, evolutionary processes (initiated by the earth) invariably take hold. No matter how many forests are cut down or automobiles constructed most of the material remains in the biosphere in some form or element. For millions of years, billions of tons of carbon were locked in geological (rock) formations in the form of coal, oil, and natural gas. With the advances of civilization, with more people and more consumption, the process interrelated in "the mechanism" will adapt to compensate for whatever humanity does—no matter what. Simply stated, the earth will take care of itself, regardless of what man does.

The earth has been struck by meteors and asteroids. Before settling into its present orbit it probably cooked like its sister planet, Venus, for at least a brief period. Little brother Mars may very well have occupied an orbit less than the 1.52 AU that it currently tracks. And the consensus among true scholars of the cosmos is that Mars may have supported life at some point in the distant past. In a strange twist Mercury is most likely the densest of the four terrestrial planets, and although the closest at only 37 million miles from the sun, is not nearly as hot as Venus. (6)

In this solar system we have a diverse group of individual planets, four rocky, two giants, two twins, and one lone wolf recently declassified as a planet, but this writer will still claim Pluto at a distance. Jupiter controls 63 moons and Saturn has 33, yet when all the calculations are tallied, the Sun commands all of their orbits. (7) The tremendous size of our sun is such that its mass is equal to 99.9 percent of the entire solar system. (8) Along with intense heat on the order of 30 million degrees Fahrenheit at the core and powerful electromagnetic fields that superheat the sun's corona, the sun is the dominant force for our solar system and especially on the inner four planets. By the time the heat has passed through several zones, temperatures have cooled to as low as 10,000 degrees Fahrenheit in the photosphere only to be superheated to 2 million degrees Fahrenheit in the corona before dispersal throughout its solar realm. (9) Along with heat, the broad spectrum of light, gamma radiation and an intense solar wind, the electromagnetic field emitted by the sun has the power to affect and even damage the earth's electrical transmission, electronic equipment, and satellites. (10) If not for the earth's own protective magnetosphere, the solar winds could strip away the earth's natural atmosphere, decimating life and leaving a lifeless planet similar to Mars.

It is the sun that governs all weather cycles and perceived phenomena, both normal and "deemed" abnormal. In all cases, contemporary scientists are limited to miniscule data in relation to the age of the planet earth. 200 years of human weather records equate to less than a blink of an eye in the annals of earth history. The often heralded high-technology ice core samples, that supposedly reveal revelations of high or low carbon dioxide levels, are not much more than a snapshot of what was probably normal for the time within the confines of the evolution of the planet AT THAT TIME. Three thousand years is not a very long time on a planet estimated to be billions of years old. Even 100,000 years would be incremental in the annals of time. The sun owns this solar system with almost all of the mass. The sun heats, illuminates, dominates with gravity, and blasts the earth with solar wind and electromagnetic waves along with powerful radiation that includes neutrinos and other sub-atomic particles. There are various other mysteries that can, in conjunction with the Sun, contribute to catastrophic weather and other planetary phenomena such as varying magnetic poles and actual pole shifts of the planet. (11) The earth wobbles during its orbit around the Sun; it is known as the precession and occurs over a period of 23,000 years. The axial tilt of the earth varies between 21.5 degrees and 24.5 degrees over a period of 41,000 years. (12) This natural gyration of the earth and the variations in the distance from the sun, combined with variable solar output within the 11-year sunspot cycle— all contribute to climatology, weather, and other earthly phenomena far beyond the influence of humans burning hydrocarbon fuels. Furthermore, as time progresses, the expansion of the heavy helium proton properties within the sun's core will continue to grow larger, increasing solar output and further changing the planetary and solar relationships in variable manifestations. (13) And yet none of the climate change or cap and trade proponents and/or scientists has mentioned these cogent facts. (14)

The planet earth was endowed with carbon, in various forms, from its inception. It is the realization of these origins that makes its use NORMAL within the confines of this geo-sphere. In the trial and error, the evolution and devolution, man must acknowledge and accept the strength and limitations of what is inherent in the inheritance of this earthly existence. This would also include the progressive knowledge base that operates in tandem with the avarice of individual desire, and usually in conflict with the collective best interests. The carbon prevalent on this planet and in this life is as natural as the respiration of air and the gravitational forces that retain all earthly matter.

The carbon tax that is proposed by world governing bodies is nothing more than an arbitrary construct devised by plutocrats to profit, control, and maximize wealth (time) for themselves. If the motives for change were really pure and genuine, then the select individuals would not be promoting such a broad-based initiative while aligning the system with personal enterprises to make billions of dollars at the expense of the poor and middle-class.

As a race of people we must accept the challenges associated with the energy systems in place and make intelligent choices with respect to stored finite sources of energy provided to us courtesy of the sun. The vast energy of the Sun, which created the energy for this planet, should be aggressively harnessed to provide a near-inexhaustible source of energy.

The sun is the source of energy that civilization must zealously adopt as the sustainable answer for dwindling finite sources that include coal and oil. The amount of energy that is absorbed by the earth's oceans and land masses from the sun in one hour is equal to all of the energy produced and consumed on the entire planet in one year. (15) Estimates of 380 billion- billion megawatts of power generated by the sun have been conservatively estimated. (16) The question then becomes why are we, as a presumably advanced civilization, not harnessing the sun to the fullest potential? One hundred, even fifty years ago, limitations in technology would have been the most plausible answer. However, today that absolutely cannot be the case. During the 1973 Arab oil embargo there were various attempts by scientists and private individuals to counteract the United States dependence on petroleum through inventions intended to harness solar energy and a host of other innovations. Many of these inventions were either purchased to be kept off the market or impeded by proponents (owners) of oil interests. Some of the same politics are still being covertly enforced today (read chapter 3).

The people that own the land where oil is produced can effectively name their price, especially when supply and demand dictate the price (profit) for oil. With the sun—no one owns the sun—it shines on everyone without monopoly.... So, in an attempt to perpetuate reliance on oil (a finite resource) elements of the government are, quite possibly, withholding valuable (advanced) solar technology from the American people.

Ever since the detonation of the first atomic bomb, humanity has made phenomenal advances in all facets of science and technology. In 1947, the sound barrier was broken in a rocket plane; just 15 years later a jet plane faster than a rifle bullet (capable of mach 3.2+) took to the skies. That airplane, the SR-71 Blackbird, was conceived and constructed by aeronautical engineers using old-school slide rules. The perils of manned space exploration are well chronicled and were revisited in 2003 with the space shuttle Columbia tragedy as the space craft was returning from a mission only to disintegrate on re-entry over Texas. This was almost exactly 17 years after the 1986 Challenger disaster, when another orbiter exploded shortly after launch. These tragedies could not erase the victories of manned space flight, such as with the landing of men on the moon on July 20, 1969, or deter continued space exploration.

Advancements in electronics, beginning in 1948 with the development of the transistor, helped set the stage for space flight and advanced computer technologies. And now, over 60 years later, there are computers that are capable of processing billions of calculations per second. Some of these computers were of necessity, to keep track of nearly 5 billion cell phones and users worldwide and the revenue generated by all the communications entailed in such a vast, complex network. (17) These same computers are the reason why human knowledge has grown exponentially over the last 40 years. By the decade of the 1990s, the sum total of man's knowledge was purportedly doubling every eighteen months. (18) In the 21st century, it is now estimated that earthly knowledge is doubling every year. By 2012, information could be doubling at an astonishing rate of just 11 hours! (19) Scientific excellence and success along technological lines are extremely evident on 21st century earth. And yet, there is limited urgency in exploiting the energy of our nearest star. This oversight is beginning to be addressed by some proponents of solar power as is evidenced by the growth and use of solar panels worldwide since 1997. (20) Photovoltaic (PV) systems have evolved to yield efficiencies of as much as 19 percent; and although much improved from the 1950s, they are still not cost competitive with fossil fuels. There are hidden factors to this reality, and the more obvious total costs of oil are not fully accounted for in the comparisons. For example, the price we pay for oil does not include the military component of insuring the flow of oil from hostile, unstable countries. The energy produced by solar technology cannot be easily impeded by politics, war, or ultimately exhausted.

The range of solar apparatus commercially available has found favor with a host of people searching for a better answer than what depleted, finite resources provide. Because of the impending eventuality with oil and coal, solar energy will have to be exploited if civilization is to survive with some semblance of the current socioeconomic model. The technology to extract the higher giga-watt energy from the sun has to exist. As previously stated, the technological advancements to date indicate that we as a people should be able to harness the power of the sun far beyond what is being accepted today. To believe that we are not sufficient in technological advancement to fully exploit solar power is simply ludicrous, and contrary to the logic of what our culture has already accomplished. The sun has the power to give life, cause cancer, mutate cells, sun-bleach away the strongest paints, and affect the most advanced electronics. Surely we can find a way to increase PV efficiencies to 70 or 80 percent with the same intellect that brought us computers, jets, genetic engineering, synthetic organs, nanotechnology, and the extension of human life in a very short evolutionary period.

Solar power has brought prominence to many empires before the United States. And it appears that one of the most revered and oft-heralded early civilizations—that of the Roman Empire—may have been locked in a very special solar cycle that influenced that empire's ascension to power. In the *Sol Invictus*, the sun's power comes to the fore among the emperors on the A.D. side of world domination. It was the soldiers' emperor, Lucius Domitius Aurelian (212-275 AD), that saved the fracturing Roman empire by evoking the soldiers' god, that of the *Sol Invictus*, or unconquerable sun. (21) The reign of Aurelian, however brief (270-275), established a pagan religious imperative that ultimately evolved into the ecumenical Christmas that is celebrated on December 25th. The sun played a clearly perceptible role in actually influencing the rise of the Roman Empire beginning in about 350 B.C. with the discernible rise in the solar maximum and extending 800 years to the ultimate fall of the empire by 476 A.D. (22) Extraordinary solar activity has been theorized to have affected birth rates through solar-genetics, whereby intense sunspot cycles influence the increased production of reproductive hormones in humans that ultimately increase births and the vitality of the progeny. (23) In an interesting paradox, the zenith of the Roman solar maxim corresponds with the height of emperor Caesar Augustus' reign (27 B.C.-14 A.D.) and the birth of Christ. (24)

All of the so-called "five good emperors," which included Nerva, Trajan, Hadrian, Antoninus Pius and Marcus Aurelius, were seemingly preordained to ride the wave of the Roman solar crest that shaped the first two centuries of the common era. Constantine The Great (274-337 A.D.) was propitiously struck by the waning photons of the Roman solar era in his adoption of Christianity and ultimately the Nicene Creed of 325 A.D. As a young man, Constantine had been an adherent to solar henotheism, the dominant religion at that time. It was a young general Constantine that, while pondering battle, looked into the sky and saw emanating from the sun a cross of light with an extra member and on one end of it a symbol similar to the letter P. That cross symbol was ultimately adopted by Constantine and was painted on the shields of his legions. The propensity to rely on chiromancy (divination) was universal among many Roman emperors, and its origins, relative to the sun god, *Sol*, served to reinforce the resolve of the legionary soldiers and the belief in their god.

Solar influences have peaked and abated with distinct patterns of profound influence over the last five millennia. These patterns, or cycles, have become more predictable and adeptly recorded with advanced scientific equipment and a modern, dedicated scientific body. The cycles of solar activity related to intense solar flares and sunspot activity cannot be discounted with respect to the influences projected on to the planet earth and its inhabitants. From the previously mentioned study of solar-genetics, we know that the sun influenced the life and death of past cultures. The Mayan civilization, and its affinity for the sun and other celestial bodies, is well documented along with various Egyptian Dynasties and that of the Sumerians. In *The Mayan Prophecies*, Adrian Gilbert and Maurice Cotterell identify and graph, in detailed solar research, how the sun influenced many aspects of the aforementioned civilization's ascension, prominence, and eventual decline through and by varying intensities of solar peaks and periods of attenuated solar output. (25)

The effects produced by the sun appear to project and affect more than the mere existence of humanity. The sun can also apparently endow certain progeny with a Midas touch. Noted author Malcolm Gladwell may have serendipitously corroborated the premise of solar-genetics endowing certain individuals, conceived during intense solar activity, with the essential power, light, or magnetic intellect that separates the "geniuses" from normal people. In his book *Outliers*, Gladwell details how many of the richest men on earth, the titans of capitalism were all born within a certain decade between the years of 1831 and 1840. (26) Of the fourteen so listed, which includes John D. Rockefeller and Andrew Carnegie, seven were all conceived during the height (1833-1837) of one of the more intense solar sunspot cycles in 300 years of recorded solar history. (27) The other seven billionaires were also immersed, at conception, with a high dose of hyper-solar particles, either at the beginning of the peak or shortly thereafter.

In addition, some of the other examples detailed by Mr. Gladwell, Bill Gates, Paul Allen, Steve Ballmer and the computer legend Bill Joy, were all conceived and born during one of the most extraordinary solar flare decades on record. (28) The period extends from 1953 (one of the hottest years on record) to 1957, which coincidentally remained the year of the highest birthrate on record for 50 years, only recently being supplanted by the 2007 record birth total. (29) The baby boom generation, those born between 1946 and 1964, were conceived and born during two of the most pronounced solar maximums on record. This observation does not diminish the peripheral cause and effects related to the end of World War II and the zenith of the industrial age.

The reverence of the sun in modern time returns to an interesting quandary related to the apt title we know as Sunday. The first day of the week, originating from the Roman holiday that was known as *dies solis* ("sun's day") was intended to be a holy day in honor of the resurrection of Christ. The first Roman emperor to embrace Christianity, Constantine, was also the first to make Sunday a legal holiday. In the purity of light and a true theological and ecclesiastical assessment, the real Sabbath day was intended to be the seventh day, which would equate to Saturday being the high day for reverence and Christian worship. Did Constantine incorporate elements of the *Sol Invictus* into his interpretation and ultimate promotion of Christianity? This calls to mind the enduring motives of an acknowledged innate human desire to pay homage to the Sun in relation to and through various religious dogmas. The Roman Catholic Church had and has tremendous influence over the strict adherence of Christian worship on the *dies Solis,* or Sunday. It is seemingly contradictory to promote the wrong day as the high-day of Christian worship. Is this a secret message or convenient reorganization of what was originally written by the prophets and scholars of old? Sun-Day speaks to us in modern times as the most segregated day of the week with respect to religious worship across a broad spectrum of faiths and cultures.

A solar cycle equates to one lap around the sun and another year older. The power of cycles gives cause to associate the orbit of the planets in this solar system around our star and ponder the similarities with the atom. When we "look" at the atom and theorize the orbit of the electron around the nucleus, we know that these constituent parts are bound by an incredible power. With the sun as the nucleus and the planets in the role of electrons, we can acknowledge the force of gravity and a microcosm on both small and grand scales. This solar system could in fact be a microcosm of the galaxy in which we reside. At a 1000-light-year distance we can be assured that our solar system looks similar to the atom we slotted in the electron microscope for perusal. The cycle of our rotating planet spinning around our favorite star compels the acceptance of the turning wheel. The wheel contributes to life on this planet in conjunction with the spinning ball of fire as our sun. Perfectly round or some measure of ellipse, the cycle governs all aspects of life as we know it. All earthly machines of necessity or pleasure require the wheel. It is the endless turning of our wheels that separates man from animal, feast from famine, war from peace, and success from failure. The cycle of empire will inexorably return to the eternal quest that ties the latent spirit of Rome to America and world dominance.

MORE BREAD AND CIRCUSES

The needs of the people and the manipulation of carnal desires, consistent in any society, were the manifestation of a conceptual and transcendent civilization that would ultimately form the basis of the American paradigm with universal effect. The rule of Rome succeeded in establishing the governmental form of the aristocracy through greed, moral nihilism, and mob control by the exploitation of basic human instincts and the minimum needs relative to human survival. The establishment of a "formal" government required ever more creative methods of citizen control beyond the lash, torture, or tip of a sword. To create order out of chaos and the structured variations of a gilded cage, control would ultimately depend on the manipulation of energy, both human and that which was relevant for the time in question: essential farm production, forest lumber for heat, horses for transport, and slaves for the aristocracy, along with the foundation of something greater than individual identity. Far beyond the premise of the once vaunted *Republic*, Rome would come to feed upon itself in its quest to achieve order and balance within a construct of patrician and plebian coexistence.

Somewhere along the river of time, it became apparent among humans that there were two distinct methods for interpersonal relations: force and reason. Before the advancement of rationale, strength was the most expedient method of persuasion. And although somewhat effective for several centuries, more tactful and logical methods became useful for the control of Roman citizens—not only in matters of procedural legitimacy, but also in maintaining the appearance of an existence that was preferable to the unknown or the pain of force. A hungry mind and an empty stomach are malleable substances in which to practice persuasion, especially when the governing body holds the means and method to encourage compliance.

Here we find that the hungry mind may, in many cases, overpower the empty stomach. The spectacle of the *Circus* personified this strange inconsistency in the human psyche, and when adeptly accompanied with *bread,* the mob became easily compliant—tamed. The motivations to gain tickets to the "games" became an overarching drive, not unlike Americans seeking tickets to the contemporary Super Bowl. But never fear, by the transmission of electrons and the advanced transistor, the games can be delivered to the peasant's efficiently through television and with more elaborate controls. This allows the Emperor(s) to invite only the wealthiest of the "patricians" to the live shows while making a nice profit. These are the newly reincarnated circuses for modern consumption, revenue generation, mob control, and, in some respects, social engineering.

The Circus Maximus and the gladiatorial shows, of the time relative to the Emperor Lucius Aurelius Commodus (161-192 A.D.), were the principle entertainment of the era. They were comparable to a modern World Series of baseball and the broad range of modern motor sports. Once known as Roman Chariot races, remarkably, the contemporary race car, track, and public preoccupation with same is clearly descendent of 1st and 2nd century Rome. (1) The Indianapolis motor speedway and Daytona stock-car race track are very similar to the main Circus Maximus race track still extant in modern Rome. When viewed from above, the center section of the race track and the large oval appear to be the principal prototype for modern race tracks. (2) But let us not forget the other circus attractions that include the dangerous sport of American football along with basketball, baseball, soccer, tennis, track and field, and the new found blood-sports such as mixed martial arts or MMA.

The new blood-sport is especially intriguing from the perspective that it is the closest reincarnation of the Roman gladiatorial games— facilitating prodigious amounts of sanguinary tissue loss during some of the most heinous fights known to modern man. The "gladiators" can legally dismember their opponent through the use of elbow punches that have opened deep gashes and could easily destroy an opponent's eye or, in a worst case, kill. Cracked ribs, along with broken arms, ankles, legs and various other bones, are the norm. In some cases copious amounts of blood actually end up being sprayed into the crowd surrounding the "Octagon." (3) The sport is not new, and similar fighting entertainment has existed in modern times in Asia for decades. With new outlets for the sport such as the Ultimate Fighting Championship (UFC) and Spike, there has been an exponential growth in the popularity of the sport; with women filling the venues in numbers rivaling the men. Famous stars such as Cindy Crawford and Pamela Anderson have been seen attending these brutal events. Beyond the normal hyperbolic rhetoric to sell tickets, there are serious "gladiators" that openly admit to trying to maim and destroy their opponents. (4)

But recall the ubiquitous electron transmission and acknowledge that such sports have the power to entertain and alter the human psyche, cheapen life, desensitize humanity, and subtly (subconsciously) encourage violence. This, in a strange irony, perpetuates the need for evolving law enforcement which validates the structure of a system that masquerades as freedom in the custom-made gilded cage for a given culture such as the United States. True freedom can never be confused with mob rule, and with a planet exceeding 7 billion people, the modern Circus Maximus will serve in pacifying components of the hungers previously mentioned. Cartoons for the little tikes, video games for pre-teens, advanced Sony PS2 and XBOX-360 and three-D for the twenty-year-olds and older, warehouses of movies—all genres, and we must consider the cell and text matrix. Imagine some teenagers that are actively entertaining themselves by texting on the order of hundreds of times per day every day. In cases of text obsession, we find news of one teen actually recording over 14,500 texts in one month. (5) Moreover, text addiction is apparently on the rise; there are clinical reports of some adolescents developing Carpal Tunnel Syndrome at ages as young as 12. One college pair endeavored to set the world record for texting by recording 217,000 texts in a single month—on a purported "unlimited" plan. The two men succeeded in breaking the old record by 35,000 texts and received a bill for $26,000 dollars. (6)

When we analyze this behavior it should be evident that a lot of communication band- width was wasted along with time, money, and energy both electric and human. But the peasants were entertained, they were monitored and charged, their circus was easily portable and the law knew where they were most of the time. By the late 1990s cellular telephones had become a major distraction in the operation of the automobile. Crashes that rivaled drunken driving collisions escalated and may have encouraged MADD to find an additional acronym as such. But this all pales in comparison to the texting driver who is on average 4 times more likely to commit vehicular homicide than that DWI suspect. Can we see a culture evolving to actually prefer pressing keys on a small illumination screen over actually talking to the intended party? It has already happened. It's the new dating fad and a dangerous contact sport when mixed with even the small 3000-pound chariots that are capable of doing tremendous damage before all of the inertia has been expended. The text fad provides a new and invigorated revenue stream for the telecommunications companies and on the periphery; we have old industries to help complement the newest addition to the ever evolving circus and a few new industries as well. Have your credit card number readily available to pay for the latest downloadable application so that the next app will work.

Another well known and highly collaborated communal circus is that of Facebook and other social networking sites such as Twitter and YouTube. Not only did these manifestations of 21st-century circus games boost personal computer sales, they provided incentive to the electron masters to craft ever smaller and more portable Blackberries, I-phones and I-pads. These new-wave devices entertain and create innovative and ever-expanding revenue streams. They also provide a method for elements in the government, like the CIA, to easily keep selected individuals under surveillance, or maybe just those close to their heart. (7) The issues of privacy and the ability of the FBI to track anyone, through the electronic tracking system of cellular phones, is being adjudicated in federal appeals court as of this writing. (8) Because of the prevalence of cell phones, including the throw-away type, and millions of surveillance cameras worldwide, the alphabet G-Men (FBI-CIA-NSA…) have all of the tools necessary to find anyone anywhere. It stands to reason that modern "entertainment" has come to serve both peasant and emperor alike. The mob is entertained (preoccupied) and the aristocracy continues to rake in untold wealth; sharing some of the bread with their employees but encouraging—sustaining— the circuses at all costs. Julius Caesar would be ecstatic in his appreciation of the modern circus; and if Commodus were alive, he would most likely have himself cloned to enable his attendance at a million games.

The speculation that all might have to wear "the mark" in order to exist in this ultra-modern civilization is made palatable through the seemingly innocuous technology of a cellular telephone. No need to mandate the tracking device, the device is the cellular telephone and has proliferated to allow access to the poor and indigent. There are literally millions of people in developing countries using their cell phones for mobile banking, even if they do not have an actual bank account. (9) In addition, the poor were able to acquire cell phones throughout the worldwide economic crises that began in 2008. (10) It must be acknowledged that someone or some group really wants everyone to have a cell phone; this includes the impoverished that lack safe and reliable water resources. No water available, but there are three signal bars and the local cell tower awaits your next telecommunications request, fascinating…

No, this writer is not denouncing the use of electronics. In fact, the technology of electron transmission and exploitation has benefited mankind in incalculable ways. Imagine being saved by a weather alert from your pre-programmed Blackberry and evading a tornado that just happened to be tracking across your exact coordinates. Hikers lost in the woods have been found through their cell phones. Phenomenal medical advancements are also attributable to electronic technology. Even with simple emergencies, the ability to easily call and communicate a request for help has saved lives. The problem(s) returns us to the issues relating to the propensity of human nature to corrupt almost anything. This maxim appears to be deeply ingrained in the human DNA and, to this point in human evolution, inescapable. The very device that helped save an accident victim miles from a hospital facility, was later the main distraction that caused an inattentive teenage driver to crash her car into the vehicle of two unsuspecting victims. (11) The insane and most odious aspect of death by cell phone is that 99 percent of the time the message transmission was trivial in nature. The protection of life and the operation of one's motor vehicle are only as important as it is conveniently arranged around the pursuit of the circus.

Incredulity aside, the preoccupation with the pursuit of pleasure, or hedonism, serves the entrenchment of the political aristocracy. In varying degrees, the diverse low, middle, and upper middle-class create cause-and-effect through their incessant desires, some innate and some manufactured by the capitalistic arm of the circus proper. It is why the commercial arm of the government will interrupt the most sacred ceremony to bring you a commercial intended to inculcate a message that is ultimately related to the circus, the games, or the continued support of the empire. Competition, along with the sport of consumption, motivates the masses that include the daughters of fashion and the sons of speed. Let us not forget the titans of capitalism, as we all must contribute through our respective passions.

Those that are not so endowed or graced with marketable talents are willing to sacrifice life and limb for a bit of fame (circus style) and a few dollars. There are circus shows where Ms. Jane Q. Public can compete in the "games" for a chance to win $50,000 to $100,000 dollars. (12) However, you may want to consider the fact that some injuries incurred while trying to make the cut may be far more life-altering than the paltry sum of money could pay for. (13) With high Nielsen ratings, the commercial arts entrepreneurs are making far more than Mr. & Mrs. John Doe off the street. (14) And the glorious reality television shows, where impromptu and purely "spontaneous" character virtues are shared with 30 million people in the coveted 7pm prime-time slot, are all-the-rave at the office cooler the next morning. (15) News flash, there can be no "real" reality where controlled, staged, and observed personal emotion is at play. It is a scientific axiom that whenever you watch an event or drama you directly, or, at the very least indirectly, affect the outcome. This would seemingly take the luster off of the word reality; or perhaps it's just an altered state of consciousness in a world of mindless television.

Speaking of altered states, the technology that makes the video games and other high-tech devices is now a part of a standard movie, or standard three-dimensional movies movie, that is. The modern computer-generated (CG) technology that goes into big-budget movies produces mind-altering effects. (16) This is a testament to video entertainment succeeding at its intended objective, occupy the masses and maybe leave a lasting message through the subliminal channels of the subconscious mind. Something along the lines of electronic anesthesia, without the outwardly negative side effects common with drugs. The elementary subliminal messages from five or more decades ago pale in comparison to the new electromagnetic visual and audio research that has been revealed, as intended, for mind control. (17) By controlling the masses with the modern circus, peaceful compliance and less bloodshed are the end result. The 3-D movies that are so in vogue in our time are the prime technology for hidden visual and audio messages to be overlaid on the normal frequencies and conveyed to unsuspecting audiences. (18) This is the potential reason for some movie patrons developing headaches and vision overload during the 3-D movies, beyond what could be attributed to individual visual abnormalities. (19)

With good entertainment come the banquet feast and the sustenance that gave reason for the Roman wise men to supply bread, oil, and some wine to the masses. The senators knew how to purchase a vote and what worked during the Roman *Republic* and later during the era of the Caesar. Food had a serious place among the Roman aristocracy and from the time of Julius Caesar onward, elaborate banquet feasts were the norm. A lingering contribution to the feasts of greats is the modern-day Caesar salad. Evidently the Roman chefs became quite adept in culinary prowess, to please the elite and maybe save their own heads. Attending the circus while eating a good meal, this had to be the earliest example of date night with "dinner and a show" and the local arenas in all their glory.

The ability to keep the mob reasonably fed goes a long way towards retaining controlling power and producing a healthy supply of soldiers to sustain the empire. The wealthy and their slaves are more willing to pay taxes to a benevolent polity that provides some of the spoils inherent in any successful empire. After a few centuries, the munificence of supplying food on the dole has consequences. By the time of A.D. 395, perhaps twenty-five-percent of the Roman Empire was on welfare. There were grain ration cards that would have to be considered the forerunner of the modern food stamp program of today. And although there were several components relative to the decline in Roman food production at the end of the empire (plague, poor farming techniques, etc), having high numbers of unproductive citizens living on the dole could not be sustained. (20)

Paradoxically the United States finds itself moving in the same direction as the late Roman Empire that has been chosen for emulation, (or perhaps dictated by the latent spirit of that power). With world-wide economic decline, we find the land of plenty, the United States, with more and more people seeking the welfare protections of the state. In the year 2010, there were more than 40 million Americans depending on food stamps to survive; this number equates to 1 in 8 households. (21) The United States would do well to remain ever mindful of the facts related to complex societies that acquire wealth and power, establish runaway budgets based on ever-increasing taxes, keep citizens preoccupied with entertainment, retain large and expensive standing armies, and fail to effectively and honestly address the limits of empire. Another interesting parallel comes to mind in association with the Roman Empire and that of the United States.

The United States learned decades ago to tax and redistribute the wealth of its citizens (subjects) to achieve cohesion with the least amount of disharmony. The more accurate description might be termed social security. Our distinguished 32nd president, Franklin Delano Roosevelt (1882-1945), appears to have been destined to be the reincarnation of a Roman Emperor. FDR was elected for an unprecedented four terms as president and ultimately became the catalyst for the 22nd amendment to the U.S. constitution. Roosevelt took the leadership role for the country at a precarious and historically relevant time in the annals of modern history. The protracted depression of the 1930s, along with the intrigue of World

War II, remains the most important elements of Roosevelt's epitaph. The societal program known as social security is once again suggestive of a Roman program previously mentioned. Franklin Roosevelt was motivated to exceed his cousin's exploits in the political arena. Theodore Roosevelt, the 26th president, had become a legend as an international foreign policy hawk and was credited with achieving supreme respect for the United States and the office of the presidency in the early years of the twentieth century. Few presidents became as popular as Theodore "Teddy" Roosevelt.

In order to make his mark and match his older cousin, FDR pushed the ambitious New Deal coalition that included initiatives that were extremely elaborate for the times. The social security act was the one program out of several fostered by the coalition to actually come to fruition (1935) and flourish as a crowning achievement by Franklin Roosevelt. The similarities of FDR to Augustus, the first Roman emperor, are striking when you compare tenure, social programs, wartime exploits, and the abiding affection that a large cross-section of the United States populace held for FDR. The image of FDR being minted on the dime coin (*denarius*) resembles, in visage, that of Caesar Augustus. The apparent semblance and countenances are preternaturally striking. (22)

Insomuch as how America came to embrace the societal programs of social security, the issue now over seventy-five years later is how to ensure the solvency of the model. With more people coming to depend on the system for retirement, the United States faces an endemic problem of millions of retired poor. No one in the Roosevelt Administration could have predicted the issues related to a 78-million baby-boom generation, the anthropology of declining birth rates among indigenous Americans, and the incessant illegal immigration problem that has created pressure on the economic structure of America. (23) Second-century Rome felt the ravages of barbarian invasion and failed to adequately address the stresses of limited resources distributed among an ever-increasing phylogenic civilization. The aging boomer generation, combined with unchecked alien consumption of government resources, can only lead to one conclusion: a dramatic devaluation of American life. (24) If we include declining energy sources or, at the very least, more expensive energy, we have the perfect storm for economic and social decline, with the inevitable collapse of the system.

But until this eventuality, the vagary of a runaway government will serve to perpetuate the control of the mob through the distribution of the daily bread. Case in point, there are multiple government agencies assigned to look out for the children through an agency once known as

AFDC or Aid to Families with Dependent Children. Originally titled Aid to Dependent Children or ADC, this social program was once highly criticized because of the perception that it encouraged teenage pregnancy and discouraged marriage. The rules originally set forth were based on outdated norms that represented a male-dominated work force and the view that women should stay home for the benefit of the child. The time period from the late 1960s into the early 1980s may have subliminally yet tacitly encouraged pregnancy so that the mother could receive government assistance and live a life "on the dole." Obviously the subsistence check was intended to keep mother and child from sleeping under a bridge with little or no food. The social implications and the dictates of an ever-expanding government to pay for this program (and others like it), created more agencies, departments, and the need for more government workers. Which (strange as it seems) motivated these new sub-agencies to justify and perpetuate their own existence. Ironically, the experiment served to imprison both parties; those in the system had little incentive to become productive participants in society and the government workers (also on the dole so to speak) liked the steady checks and benefits offered by Uncle Sam. The aforementioned program had a serious restructuring in 1996 under President Bill Clinton's administration. The changes included a new title to TANF or Temporary Assistance to Needy Families. The new agency also had limits that pleased Mr. and Mrs. Taxpayer. This coincidentally pushed many government workers to vie for jobs in the new agency and associated offices, a recurring theme, to be sure.

The Department of Health and Human Services has over 160 agencies and support offices under its jurisdiction. That is a prodigious number of government employees to provide the social framework for the individual cradle-to-grave oversight that serves the evolving dictates of the aristocracy. The enormous dedicated budget to operate the social services leviathan in the United States paid out over $650 billion dollars in Social Security benefits in 2009 alone. (25) The true measure of the U.S federal government budget is truly an enigma cloaked in illusion. The U.S. government debt clock continuously updates to portend an imploding mountain of debt that will invariably lead to financial and social devastation. (26) As of this writing, the United States brings in over $2-trillion dollars in taxes annually but future annual entitlements exceed the $14-trillion mark. The inability to effectively pay even the interest on such a vast sum demands a dramatic reconciliation in the not too distant future. The final recompense for such an elaborate pyramid could manifest itself in a number of horrible eventualities.

When it comes to entertaining the masses, money is no object. The titans of capitalism count on and reinforce the tradition of our ancestors by making all our holiday wishes a tribute to the rule. The economy of the United States is driven by passion(s). As a consequence some of the most revered dates entrenched in our Roman calendar also generate untold wealth for those that are passionate about a certain Saint named Valentine. It is a statistical fact that the top American holidays, in both revenue generation and participation, are derived from the Roman Empire. An insightful view of the second most celebrated day in the United States; that of St. Valentine's Day, identifies a broad-based universal appeal. (27)

Even a misanthrope may participate in the ritual of selecting, or being selected, as the object of Love interest—if only for an ephemeral episode. The true lovers will renew and reaffirm their love by some act of giving; and on a holiday dedicated to lovers, the measure of that love will be affirmed in units of life energy. And this is of special concern for the capitalistic and merchant faction of not only America, but the world. Billions of dollars of greeting cards are purchased and mailed, millions more in roses and gifts, and chocolates, and expensive meals, and the intrigue that accompanies most amorous activity. (28) Our school children are encouraged to embrace the high ceremonial day of love at a young age. Perhaps we are all just paying tribute to a latent culture that still influences and commands the passions of those once enthralled— possessed by the circus game. The sweetness of the intended benevolence is apparently lost on the purported martyr or martyred saints that prompted Roman Catholic Pope Gelasius I, to establish the feast of St. Valentine in 496 A.D. The perennial holiday of February 14 is designated as the day *Valentinus* was entombed in a suburb of Rome. A complex holiday from all accounts, the very fact that a holiday is dedicated to the passion of love speaks to a transcendental spirit that supports the innate human drive for procreation. The pleasure of making love is neither lost in translation nor wasted on the hedonist.

The rule of love is deeply entrenched in the latent yet obvious influences associated with the late Roman Empire. In the literary world, semantics can be articulated on the order of multi-dimensional physics and nearly as complicated. And there are those that would question the assertion, but the English language is derived from a compilation of many of the great and past civilizations. Greece readily comes to mind and there is the complexity of Latin. A note of limited disclosure on the words relative to the language of Love: romance, roman-tic, and even the word romanticism return us to the ubiquity of our ROMAN ancestral legacy.

Modern-day bread and circuses are far more complicated than the agrarian, animal, and slave energy that propelled past civilizations. The complexity of the 21st century perpetuates controlled chaos and the requisite maintenance of the circus that has something for everyone and everyone for the passion (comfort) that the circus emanates. The pursuit of the circus is conservatively fifty-percent of the entire world's commercial and gross domestic product. And in a strange convoluted manner, the impetuous and driven passion encourages invention, which spurs ever more invention and the inevitable consumption. Through the unlimited passion of desire and constant exposure, the moral and basic human instincts become altered, primarily through the collective conscience of a given society. This has been studied at length and is known in numerous sociological disciplines with terms such as group-think, herd mentality, mob hysteria and the like.

How are the children? The answer leads us to examine the realities of raising the child through remote control—television remote, that is. In the United States our children have more in common with the television in their room than with their parents. The average child spends almost twice as much time watching television as attending school and a reported 54 percent of young children would rather watch television than spend time with their fathers. (29) This electronic preponderance has influenced the emotional and psychological development in children, with mostly negative results. Excessive TV perusal among children has contributed to increased childhood obesity. (30) There are studies that have charted a definitive rise in childhood diabetes and coronary heart disease in pre-teens over the last thirty years. (31) This is an ominous correlation, tied not only to excessive television but also to video and computer games that have become the principal companions of our children. Even more foreboding are the studies related to the number of murders and violent acts that children observe on television during their most influential (significant) developmental years.

The constant exposure to murder has to have some effect on the child's emotional perspective and the sanctity of life. If a child witnesses 8000 murders on television by the time that child is 12 years old, this would equate to two murders per day for every day of life the child has lived. (32) Because the mind of a child is not sufficiently developed to fully discern dramatic theatre from civilized humanity, certain schisms in the child's mind are bound to manifest themselves through imitation and more. The age of the child, along with the moral and relative teachings of the parents, ultimately contributes to a range of variables in the child's disposition. Recall that in many cases it is the television that serves as teacher, companion, and perhaps moral arbiter for the child.

Over the last twenty years there has been an increased incidence of murder perpetrated by children. In many cases those killed were by the use of firearms. The availability of firearms in the American home (unlocked) may contribute to the alarming statistics, however, not all of the young murderers used guns. In the case of a 2-year-old toddler, the boy may have just been mimicking something he saw on television when he shot and killed his 9-year-old brother. (33) In other cases some type of abuse, and the possibility of the activity being revealed, contribute to the motivations of murder. A 14-year-old California boy found himself in just such a predicament when his 4-year-old victim threatened to tell his mother of being molested by the teen. No gun was needed; the larger, stronger teenager simply drowned the boy in the bathtub and hid the body in the clothes dryer. (34) There are also the age-old motivations of jealousy. In Pittsburgh, PA we find an 11-year-old boy, so threatened by his father's new love interest that he planned and carried out the murder of his prospective stepmother by shooting her with his own 20-gauge shotgun while she slept. The boy then calmly got on a school bus and was arrested at school a few hours later. Incidentally, the boy's victim was eight months pregnant. (35)

And then there are the more nefarious examples that tend to support the theory of too much negative inculcation (television murder) contributing to a heinous crime. In Jefferson City, MO, a 15-year-old girl killed a 9-year-old neighbor girl—just to know what it felt like to kill someone. The teenaged killer evidently premeditated the murder; this was determined after the pubescent suspect admitted to digging two shallow graves before strangling, cutting, and stabbing the victim to death. (36) There are apparently few limits as to how young a child might premeditate murder; such was the case with an 8-year-old boy that had purportedly been spanked "1000 times" and had decided to kill his father and roommate to preclude any additional corporal punishments. (37) The young boy shot both his father and friend from a distance with a .22 caliber rifle. There are many more examples, and undoubtedly whole books focused on this singular subject have been written.

From the murderous barbarism of millennia ago, we as "civilized" people have come full circle in our pursuit of a social existence that could support seven or ten billion people (spirits) with room to spare and everyone with sufficient bliss to warrant the support of the circus. The instinctive code within the very DNA of Homo Sapiens apparently commands the perpetual spilling of blood so that others might live within multiple spectrums of existence. The Roman Empire continuously sought war and conquest. The United States, whether justified or subject to interpretation, uses the same model. On the battlefield or in the arena, the incessant thirst for blood is part and parcel to the perpetuation of empire. This is why we willingly nurture the lust for blood in competition, kingdom building, and the birth of fresh warriors. In 44 B.C., Julius Caesar was viciously slashed, hacked, and stabbed to death. So enamored with the knife and cutting, our brothers and sisters of the healing arts perfected and promoted the modern en vogue technique for delivering our children. It is called the cesarean section (named for Julius Caesar).

There are some historians that will challenge the assertion as unsubstantiated. However, references by Roman historian, Pliny the elder, relating a story of Julius Caesar's birth or relative being born through surgical technique are of tangential merit. (38) It is the way J.C. died that is the lasting imprint of bloodshed relative to not only life—but death as well. Which may tend to answer the question of why there have been ever-increasing incidents of Caesarean section births worldwide over the last century. In the United States caesarean births have been on the rise since 1985. By 1996 the United States rate of caesarean births had climbed to 28 percent, which equates to one in four births. (39) It is during and throughout the early 1990s to date that many of the children that have contributed to the escalating child-murder rate were born. In other words, as caesarean births have increased so has the child-murder rate—which would presumably include a percentage of the perpetrators being brought into the world through the name of Caesar. The surgical technique has its purpose for saving the mother and child during a difficult childbirth or other health-related issues, e.g. uterine rupture, breech, prolapsed cord, and a number of other potentially life-threatening complications. The procedure has been aggressively adopted in many areas of the world where the mother(s) could have had the baby naturally—and opted not to. This has some people asking why, especially with the desire (question) of some mothers wanting to attempt normal vaginal birth after having had a caesarean section. (40)

For some as-yet-undiscovered reason, the women in Italy have a particularly high incidence of caesarean sections. In one province, 60 percent of births were by caesarean section in 2008. In the areas near and around Rome, the rate is above 44 percent and is purported to be as high as 85 percent in some private medical facilities. (41) It appears that Julius Caesar, whether accurately warranted or not, left an endearing impression and legacy on his native descendants with respect to the knife, blood, birth and death through surgical technique.

The passion of Caesar, and more acutely the Emperor and his excesses, give cause to contemplate the true origins of dramatic theatre. From the west we have the variable passions displayed at will for those enamored with the art of pretense. Through celluloid or other related electrons, we are able to look deeply into the soul of our chosen thespians and take comfort in an elected human emotion that evokes the essence of our carnal desires. So enamored are we all with the tinsel of Hollywood and for that which might salaciously delight the senses and bring peace to that aspect of our tormented psyche. Perilous and taut, how the subconscious mind might lead us to open a door of dreadful content in the most feared corridor of our hidden conscious. *There they were the brightest stars on a moon-lit night, just below the hallowed sign in the Hollywood hills…*

If the entire world's a stage then surely Rome had a hand in that conception. Some will deny the contributing thespian antics of Nero Claudius Caesar Augustus Germanicus (37-68 A.D.). Of all the emperors, Nero must be acknowledged as one of the top ten, if merely for his contribution to the performing arts. Some of the recurring assertions of Nero fiddling while Rome burned have been refuted using CSI-style investigations. For one thing, there were no musical instruments comparable to a violin in Nero's time, and the lyre may not have been as convenient to strum and avoid the burning embers while entertaining the most devout of his retinue. One thing is certain; Nero had a serious affinity for the performing arts—all types. (42) It is believed that Nero was seduced by the notion that a performing artist, could, in effect, become immortal through the lasting adoration of the artists' fan base. And this admiration would endure throughout all eternity. (43) There is evidently some truth to this if we examine the adulation that is afforded Hollywood's "A-list" movie stars. Let's face it, anyone that can make $20 million dollars or more for a single movie, while simply pretending to be someone else, should be exalted and glorified in starry, god-like fashion…

This, in many ways, is far superior to being an emperor. No need for soldiers to enforce any mandates, you simply show up for a red-carpet event and the throngs of worshippers blindly submit to your every whim. You are even afforded special privileges outside the normal boundaries known as laws. The local police captain may be a fan, and the district judge needs an autograph for an extra-special teenaged son or daughter. Hollywood is indeed a dimension all its own. It pays homage to Rome by identifying every movie production in the chronology of the Roman numerals. As you look to the sky and ponder the twinkling of your favorite star—know how well the theatre and the circus are all one as the scion of Rome.

THE PHILOSOPHY OF TRUTH

If beauty is in the eye of the beholder then surely truth and its attendant reality can be expressed by those that own the laws and conventions of composite truth. This truth, or the perception of same, is surely a nebulous notion. Before complex religion, the force of will in the religion, the dominant party dictated all truth or the forced illusion customary at that point in time. To acknowledge truth one must be able to sift through the pretention and comfort afforded one's self when no one else truly knows your thoughts. The art of persuasion that exists among the most celebrated actors may only briefly compare to the posture and eloquence portrayed by you for some significant other. And yet we are convinced that the elements of truth—this composite truth will sufficiently legitimize an existence thought to be real even if controvertible evidence and mortal doubt conspire to collapse the construct. Thoughts of a certain realization you may have embraced as truth, only to later discover it was all a lie or an elaborate conundrum. The illusion is designed to be more palatable, especially for the author of the story.

Here is an interesting paradox: a philosopher will fiercely promote a doctrine or ideology that has many of the same hallmarks of a fervent religious belief. Some could say that Martin Luther was a philosopher in monk's clothing, and that perhaps John Stuart Mill was the true theologian in this juxtaposition. No irreverence is intended and since beauty, or truth, may be unique to the prospective beholder, well; perhaps you will comprehend the intended message. We may hear what we want and see what heralds all pleasure, so much for the immediacy of gratification. The quest to possess one's rightful share of what was endowed by creation and the proxy of our orbiting sphere stands in fleeting insurrection and beyond the limits of the mere mortal. Share it, will it, but be advised of the illusion of the possession. The truth demands a certain acceptance that will never be negated by legislative committee.

To be a true lover of knowledge one must be willing to suspend personal vices and emotional impulses to understand the intellect of reason. The masters of old may have been, in some ways, better suited than modern man to channel, without distraction, that aspect of the human mind that makes man the supreme animal. The pre-Socratic philosophers have only recently been truly acknowledged for their contribution to the most profound questions and drives that compel us as a race of beings first, animals, homo-sapiens, and humans last, but not least. The great minds of antiquity that reasoned the earth and related materials were indeed composed of very tiny particles that were attracted and repulsed at the same time has been, in recent decades, soundly affirmed through scientific trial and relentless inquiry. A wise Greek by the name of Empedocles (490-430 B.C.) theorized that Love and Hate (attraction and repulsion), two of the most profound forces driving human existence, had to exist in all matter, and ultimately this was later found and defined in the sub-atomic realm. (1)

Socrates (470-399 B.C.), as is widely known, may have been the chief catalyst for the title of philosopher. But he had some serious contemporaries, one of which, Democritus the atomist (460-370 B.C.), is only now being recognized as one of, if not the, first philosophers from antiquity to actually postulate that matter is in fact formed and constructed of tiny particles we now denote and accept as atoms. This man did not have an electron microscope or potential (electric) energy to assist or comfort him in his drive to utilize the power of the human mind. These real-deal philosophers had time to really think hard—without major distraction—and come up with some intellectual insights that tend to irrefutably cancel out some later-day philosophers that are (were) driven by self-aggrandizement. Socrates separates the foundational era of profound thought from those that were so deeply influenced by Plato, and later his student Aristotle. The purity of introspection, which was the hallmark of Socrates, cannot be overstated.

In order to "know thyself" in the tradition of Socratic doctrine, one must be able to face the first horrid truth of human existence, that being mortality. (2) The limits of this mortal existence compel us all to acknowledge a finite life and thusly, a serious limit on what a human could possibly, truly know, empirically or otherwise. What is known or believed may indeed be characterized by epistemology, which, simply stated, equates to questions about knowledge. An interesting paradox crashes the party and leaves in its wake questions about the questions and whether or not human consciousness is simply "thinking about thinking." We know that at various points along a time line, thought was put into action and many things—right or wrong, ethical or existential, came into being in the nature of human reality. And with this realization, the idea of innate knowledge became the doctrine of innatism. (3) This philosophy was promoted by Plato (428-347 B.C.) and was a departure from his mentor and teacher, Socrates. Unlike his idealistic professor, Plato was strict and authoritarian in his life and in his approach to human intellectual actualization.

Originally named Aristocles at birth, Plato chose to distinguish himself from his revered teacher by disagreeing with Socrates on a serious point: Plato chose to apotheosize the philosopher, so much that he is the principal luminary in his seminal work *The Republic*. The premise of *The Republic* sets in place a society of definitive class divisions consisting of the highest class, the Philosophers, followed by the Warrior class, and lastly the Producer class. The philosopher class are revered and considered to be intellectually endowed, the foremost of all human creation. The warriors are naturally (inherently) protectors and are designated to protect the state. The lowly producer class (perhaps code for slave) will contribute to the goods and services, another term for gross domestic production... Plato's ideal social and quasi-political state, upon first perusal, seems eerily similar to a hybrid aristocracy with invidious class warfare a perpetual probability. Some would say this is intended to preclude the mob mentality of the dreaded democracy. From Plato's perspective it was an out-of-control democracy that contributed to the demise of his teacher and mentor, Socrates. Human foibles, including the emotion of envy, may have incited much of the hate directed at such a larger-than-life figure. And from this storied chapter in antiquity we see a pattern in the design of society intended to give rationale to social classes for some purely emotional or egocentric ulterior motive. (4)

The Republic could be acknowledged as a master plan for an "ideal"society. And although many have promoted the idea of a Utopian society, where class divisions would be accepted and nurtured, no such beneficent panacea has yet to emerge. If we are to fully embrace the ideology of the innate knowledge within human beings, then the fallacy of a Utopia should be academic. The thoughts of some of the most revered minds are (were) still in a minority in the grand scheme. During the time of the aforementioned great minds, there may have been a few million people sharing a seemingly vast planet at that time. A brilliant idea or charismatic spirit would undoubtedly stand out, even without the help of CNN. Those who were inclined to have their own visions for a better world may very well have embraced their ideas and thoughts as superior. In choosing a divergent path, contrary to what was accepted by the mob, someone or some group could and would invariably create friction, tension, and even war. Now multiply this scenario by fifty million, or five hundred million, or seven billion, and well, you get the idea.

Here is a contradiction that, on one hand, makes Plato great in his own right, yet clueless in that other realm. Plato theorized and spoke exhaustively about the innate knowledge in human beings. He was zealous in imparting the vision of an awakening consciousness in his famous "The Cave" analogy. This tutorial was a metaphor to exemplify how most people live within a very narrow band of conscious reality, never really knowing the full scope of their existence until they free themselves of their chains and partake in the light that is outside of their comfort zone. Plato is correct in this assessment and his impassioned belief is constantly being proved by virtue of the relentless stream of ideas, inventions, discoveries and insights into human consciousness. There had to be some innate intelligence for there to have been any advancement in civilization(s). Scientists have experimented with reactions of infants and have effectively proven that a newborn baby, within a few days of being born, is able to identify its mother through sight. (5) And even with the broad variations in cultures, there are similar underpinnings in a wide range of similar societies, and this speaks to the commonality of the human condition— regardless of culture, race, ethnicity, or global location. There have been some scientists and closet philosophers that have attempted to refute this observation. However, these individuals would be required to admit their own deficiency with respect to human emotions and mortal flaws that may include ethnocentrism.

In a certain context, classicism is insidiously destructive by reason of its broad-based and ecumenical pervasiveness. The multiple classes of poor and very-poor invariably contribute to a rift of antagonistic opposition that can and does exist among even the most down trodden. The heralded rich, or if you prefer affluent, will painstakingly attempt to differentiate themselves in any number of ways. And the various artists or successful business entrepreneurs may or may not consider themselves, on par, legitimate equals. We must also include those of certain bravado, or shall we say incendiary spirit, who tend to make the absolute best instruments of war. This is a minor sub-text in the ideology of Plato, as he theorized *The Republic* and as it was recorded and promoted in his intellectual magnificence. This set the stage for multiple civilizations to follow the pattern, with the nearest chronologically significant civilization being the montage of Greco-Roman influence. And this ultimately became the monolithic Roman Empire, allowing and creating variations of the Plato *Republic* model. (6) *"I pledge allegiance to the flag of the United States of America and to the republic for which it stands...."*

It is rational to associate some relevance to Plato's Republic in the latter manifestations of the Roman Empire. Perhaps subtly at first and two centuries before the Punic wars, Rome and the quest for world supremacy would have drawn from models of the most heralded minds and intellectual theories of that time—in this case the three inimitable wise men and native sons of Greece. And the influence of our wise men would have been as a Saturn Five rocket, with each successive stage further propelling their combined philosophical dogma and social designs deep into the consciousness of generations for centuries. Although it would be one hundred years before the third of the triumvirate, Aristotle (384-322 B.C.), would add to the contagious influence of philosophy, his weight proved to be nearly as profound as his master's. His instruction of the military genius, Alexander the Great, pales in comparison to the duality of the reverence for his teacher and the definitive antithesis that would ultimately be studied by vast numbers of subsequent philosophers to follow. In simplest terms, Plato had an intense mystical component inherent in his intellectual reasoning; and Aristotle, his eminent pupil, emerged as the high priest of empiricism. (7) Spirit-filled mysticism and the doctrine of objectivity generally do not mix. This is perhaps the main divergence between a disciplined philosopher and the most devout theologian.

The personal revelations by Plato that are attributed to the trilogy of classes, necessary for an advanced society to function, were purportedly derived from the personal introspection of the philosopher. According to Plato, the primary elements inherent in the human soul could be defined as: *wisdom* (the philosopher), an *active spirit* (the warrior and seeker of conquest), and the *appetites* (the desire and need for consumption). The last facet, inherent in all humans, is exponentially magnified with an ever-expanding population and successful civilizations.

As the philosophers (kings, judges, bankers, entrepreneurs and warmongers) came to the full realization of what the demands of a civilization entailed and the many ancillary components needed to make the model function, hybrid forms of Plato's Republic became a reality. One noteworthy example speaks to the three principles embodied in the philosophic realm. Socrates could easily fit the form of active spirit; Plato would garner the most votes for the sage of the group; and Aristotle was infinitely more attuned to the desires and appetites cogent in the reality of a material world. The three stages of a given civilization, that being-- (inception and growth, maturity and devolution, and old age and decay) seem remarkably like a mortal life. Further insights reveal what is representative of a government that would distribute the power of governance through three distinct entities, Emperor, senate, and patrician. Closer to modern-day reality, the executive, judicial, and legislative branches of government come to personify, on a tangible level, the human components that drive humanity as it was articulated by Plato. The government, along with big business, is tempered by the military or, in the case of the United States, the military-industrial complex. The trilogy of the essential elements, necessary for an idea, organism, or culture to survive, is all strangely interdependent with respect to consumption and passion. The insights rendered from such an all-encompassing revelation by Plato surely tempered his approach to philosophy and the esoteric nature of the subject. And although some of the examples written herein are far more complex than can be briefly elucidated, the challenge for the reader is to identify those examples most relevant within their respective domain.

During the late third century B.C., the dominance of Roman expansion would have undoubtedly sought a framework to ensure some cohesion among the patricians and plebeians. The inherent passions that Plato had identified invariably contributed to the fledgling Republic through adaptation and the influences that were contributed by Aristotle. For with Aristotle, objective relativism may have guided his political inclinations for purely personal reasons. Aristotle came from money and even the subtle sway of riches, and a lofty title, would have to be weighed in light of the animus he felt after being passed over for the title vacated at the time of Plato's death. With the formal logic approach established by Aristotle, the ability to advance any and all issues associated with society would be devoid of sensitivity and the humanistic moral code. This is not an outright condemnation of Aristotle; however, there are some historians that would assert that his doctrines related to political policy and expedience predate those of Niccolo Machiavelli. That's right, Aristotle may very well have been the model for the dreaded blood-thirsty tactics (sometimes required in Machiavellian doctrine) in order to establish a polity and obtain or remain in power. (8)

By the time Aristotle had died in 322 B.C., the Roman Empire was well on its way to becoming the world power. The Etruscan, Umbrian, and Gaul wars of 283 B.C. were merely primers for the first Punic Wars that lasted over 130 years; with Carthage ultimately coming under complete Roman subjugation in 133 B.C. The many variations in a structured empire, incorporating many of the models suggestive of Greece's favorite sons, would have invariably been implemented in various regions conquered by the wave of Roman imperial expansion. As previously written, in all facets the figurehead (or heads) dominated in conjunction with a warrior class and an ever-growing labor or slave class that served to supply the empire for several centuries. The command structure of scholarly patricians, proconsuls, and military men would have had some level of formal education, and those lessons included the teachings of our three wise men, especially Plato and his protégé, Aristotle. We begin to see at the 100 B.C. marker a form of philosophy more attuned to that of a dreamer or mystical entity. The Hellenistic Age would have been past its zenith, with Greek culture and philosophical doctrines broadly disseminated. Religion (in various forms) would have existed for some time long before the rise of Rome as the dominant world power. But we begin to see a marked increase in its comingling of the "religious" factions and the wise philosophers before the event marking the birth of Jesus Christ.

The polytheism of mythological gods prevalent during the Hellenistic period would have greatly contributed not only to the Greek culture pervasive in the Mediterranean, but also among the Roman conquerors. The Romans are widely known to have adopted many customs and practices of the various cultures they subjugated. Religion, along with the Greek philosophy prominent in that realm, was no exception. It is widely known that many of the mythical gods pervasive in Greek culture were assumed by the Romans and the names were changed to suit the Roman ideal (identity). Here is where the fusion of religion and philosophy most assuredly began to feed off of each other; provoking questions, introspection, and the search for answers to a world that was tenuous at best and savagely blood-thirsty at its worst. The mystical and sometimes comforting perception of a higher-power may have been soothing for those lost in the pain and numbness of constant upheaval. Could philosophy be considered masculine and religion more definitively feminine? In the search to understand the dichotomy of the two, this speculation is equally as valid as another—in the grand scheme, and for lovers of knowledge. There came a time when it was far safer to espouse philosophy over religion; with the earliest persecution of those belonging to the "supreme being" by the conflicting invidious nature of the governors and later the Caesars. Philosophy had origins from mere mortals; the idea of origin, relative to a supreme being, is much more difficult to control or legislate. From this perspective, the revelation that there may not be anything stronger than a belief is the principal imperative linking religion and philosophy. And the question of assigning human characteristics to each is not outside the realm of mortal comfort and acceptance. This becomes even more apropos when you take a close look at the structure and inclinations inherent in the Roman Catholic Church. There is the profound emphasis on the Virgin Mary and later, Mary the Mother of God. This unique dogma in Roman Catholic Christian theology commands an analysis when aligned with the proposition of philosophy being the masculine and religion acting as the feminine manifestations of the most complex motivating preoccupations in human existence.

The quest for human understanding began to make the connections of philosophy and religion from the earliest days of the A.D. side of recorded history. A Roman philosopher named Plotinus (205-270 A.D.) is credited with the first efforts to marry the temporal and the spiritual through what came to be known as Neoplatonism. It has been classified as pagan monotheism, which, strange as it may be interpreted, contributed to the intensification of Christianity through direct (and some would say fierce) competition for at least two centuries. (9) The other competing religions of the time included Gnosticism, which would be ideally suited for the most ardent philosophers of the time. Plotinus may have been merely a zealous adherent of Platonic doctrine and the positive contribution of recognizing the importance of both belief systems may very well have hastened the acceptance of religion and Christianity through the efflorescent channels of reason.

In the acknowledgement of Plotinus, his contemporary Origen (185-254 A.D.), deserves honorable mention for his contributing promotion of philosophical reasoning combined with Christian religion. Origen paid a high price for his beliefs and the promulgation of same. Roman Emperor Decius had him jailed and severely tortured, which led to his death. One hundred years later, one of the greatest Christian philosophers that ever lived came forward to give additional foundational reason to Christian theology. Augustine of Hippo (354-430 A.D.) gave rationale to the teachings of Plato in conjunction with Church theology, and in this virtue found middle-ground with respect to the elders in the church and the associated dogma. The arguments postulated by Augustine were profound enough to give even an atheist cause to ponder the most philosophical questions of the time. And although only 70 or so years removed from the reign of Constantine The Great, religious persecution would have still existed in a rapidly deteriorating Western Roman Empire. The philosophy of stoicism, which had reigned among the Roman elite, would not be easily extinguished. Combine this with the lingering pervasiveness of Gnosticism and it becomes easy to envision such a cold and calculating indifference that had been bred into the Roman culture, and the hubris befitting a world imperial power. This overwhelming pride could not be easily swayed lest the supernatural should make its presence felt.

The power of the Supreme Being is intended to be beyond the comprehension of mere mortals; this may read as academic… and, even facile for the informed mind. Plotinus, as an adherent of Plato's doctrine, came to accept and promote the principle of emanation—the life force of God. This doctrine was derived through adaptation and the comingling of Neoplatonism and aspects of Christianity along with the new spiritual belief systems. It is from this foundation that Saint Augustine would open the discussion of the Supreme Being as irrefutable. Speaking with a candor and reverence that was unassailable, Saint Augustine set the foundations of divine grace, predestination, and the sovereignty of the Supreme Being from insights learned from his predecessors and his involvement in heightened conflicts between theologians and ecclesiastics. Saint Augustine was a gifted and prolific writer and he used these skills, and his courage, in confronting issues of reason and religion on similar planes of informed thought. He may very well have sought quiet compromise in political and theological contests—ultimately appealing to deep-seated innate human morality. (10) This may have been subconsciously suggestive in his autobiography known as the *Confessions*. By acknowledging his own mortal shortcomings, in conjunction with the salvation espoused in Christianity, Saint Augustine won over holy men and neophyte Christians alike. Saint Augustine routinely returned to the Bible and in particular the Book of Romans. The scriptures related to improving one's character, avoiding adulterants, and living a life of purpose, motivated Augustine to become the best Christian possible. (11) His work related to the denunciation of pagan rituals and the religion of pantheism brought him much acclaim.

Saint Augustine happened along at a propitious moment in time—not just for the wave of hunger driving the proliferation of Christianity, but the beginnings of the most pervasive and powerful church the world had yet to engage. In the year 383, Christianity became the official religion of the Roman Empire by the decree of Emperor Theodosius I; this is also about the time that Augustine made his official conversion to Christianity. The Roman Catholic Church may have existed in some form from the original Confession of Peter, dating from shortly after the death of Christ, and Peter as his successor within the context of specific Bible scripture. (12) With the Emperor on the side of the Church, the die was cast to promote the exponential growth of the Roman Catholic Church. The powerful writings and teachings of Saint Augustine would come to be adopted by Catholic elders and skillfully promulgated (marketed) in conjunction with the captive church law of Rome. Through concerted effort and support of the polity, the Roman Catholic Church could develop theological doctrines tempered by philosophy and through various techniques create a universal religion that would come to be axiomatic in its appeal and advance the Imperial dominance of Rome. After centuries of war and bloodshed, Rome would come to exploit religion as a tool of control and domination through the power of a belief—slowly at first, but ultimately taking root in the grand scheme of control through affiliation with the Supreme Being and procuring wealth at the same time. The very word, Catholic, means universal in scope, and is generalized in a broad cross-section of world-wide personal appeal. Such a broad-based appeal assuredly was influenced by the competing beliefs of the times. These various belief systems would have included elements tied to the aforementioned Gnostics.

Most scholars of religion agree that Gnosticism flourished during the second and third centuries A.D. and posed a direct challenge to Christian orthodoxy. The quest for understanding the nature of reality, human drives, and the belief in forces of extraordinary power, compelled many to search all viewpoints in acquiring knowledge. Gnosis or "revealed knowledge" gave cause to ponder the notion of man being on a level with God with respect to knowledge. This may have been an erroneous supposition based on the Old Testament account of Adam and Eve eating from the tree of knowledge and believing what was portrayed by the serpent in the Garden of Eden. And although it is safe to say there are multiple dynamics to consider, one thing is sure: there was an intense and collaborative effort to eradicate the "heretics" that were a threat to the orthodox religion based on Christianity. Gnosticism was intimately intertwined with Christianity in the early days of its expansion, 80-200

A.D., and would have been aggressively denounced as the age of the institutional church came to power. (13) The established hierarchy of priests and deacons, along with bishops acting as absolutes and guardians of the closed orthodoxy, were too much for the Gnostics to overcome. The various factions of the religion were not sufficiently organized to fight the relentless attacks of the Orthodox Church. If factions of the Gnostics were affiliated with established Christianity, it stands to reason that elements of the religion may very well have developed a stealth mind-set, in order to survive the inquisitions and heretical persecutions.

This perspective provides motive to ponder the true amalgam of the "universal" house of worship known as the Roman Catholic Church. As acceptance of religion and Christianity grew, there had to have been compromise in recognition of paganism across a broad spectrum. The religion of thought and knowledge that had also been known as philosophy now had new corridors to acceptance and promotion by the laws associated with Christianity and the church. The Gnostics became Christian philosophers and through the practice of their esoteric knowledge, subtly and progressively they would come to employ their influence in any number of ways. To further understand the premise, the priests that were highly regarded for promotion within the church were required to obtain graduate degrees that included the extensive study of philosophy (the practice still exists today). And it becomes apparent why the proliferation of the monasteries was so widespread during the middle-ages.

The age of monasticism heralded the intensive evolution of philosophical reason with Christianity as the conveyance of a deliberate and unassailable dogma. At the edge of the dark ages, the motives to retreat to the confines of the monastery and become engrossed in the pursuit of the Supreme Being would have a special appeal. Noted theologians would have envisioned the ultimate coenobitic commune to be self-sustaining and religiously all-inclusive. However, quiet reflection would be routinely disrupted by the cacophony of conflicts in establishing the one true church. The latent controversies posited by Valentinus and his Gnostic faction would not go peacefully into the night. With counter religions questioning the live resurrection of Christ, and the purported *Gospel of Truth* attributed to Valentinus, the orthodoxy had much work to do. And here again, Rome made a brilliantly strategic move to establish "The Church" and suppress any competing ideologies or alternative views on the Supreme. (14)

With the deterioration of the Western Roman Empire, especially after 476, the objectives relative to absolute power would be found in the recesses of the mind. The philosophical process of strategic thought, including conspiratorial design, would invariably be used to establish the church, its dogma and ecumenical pervasiveness. A peripheral benefit would include phenomenal wealth from which to influence all manner of earthly inducements. Entities in the church sphere had grasped the potential power of religion to influence society in general and civilization as a whole. Rome had tapped into this psychology in the nationalistic pride it inculcated into its citizens; so much so that the barbarians that had been conquered in previous centuries now returned with the intent of being formally accepted as Roman citizens. This knowledge was used by subsequent popes and other religious leaders to placate and alter the fierce indignation of various barbarian hordes through the late fifth and sixth centuries.

Beginning with Saint Augustine, the Roman Catholic Church crafted and promoted the missionary model that would establish various religious communities and learning centers intended to disseminate Christian dogma, morals, and norms that would ultimately become tradition. The Augustinian monastic example would ultimately be the precursor for all of the noteworthy iconic theologians to follow. And although the first Order of Saint Augustine could be more accurately identified as the mendicant friars, it was the times in question that called for the order to be more fluid and itinerant in spreading the word of God.

As surely as Augustine was the prototype saint and foremost theological mind, the arrival of Benedict of Nursia (480-547) would decisively bring the Roman Catholic Church—and its preeminence—center stage for the entire world. The mysteries surrounding Benedict are multi-faceted and complex. His Benedictine Order would come to be the monastic standard for emulation and ultimately influence the early middle or dark ages immediately following the decline of the Roman Empire. In fact, for a number of reasons, the time period of 550 to 1150 has been commonly referred to as the "Benedictine centuries" and with justification. (15) For a man that purportedly had little desire to cast the light of fame upon him, Benedict's piety and genuine quest to be one with God could not be ignored, much less unacknowledged. The original twelve monasteries that were built by Saint Benedict (including the famous Monte Cassino) would pay supreme dividends in the promotion of the monastic system and the Roman Catholic Church.

A descendant of Roman lineage, Benedict turned away from a rich life of privilege to embark on a solitary quest to become one with his God.

He lived alone in a cave for years and was eventually approached, with reverence, by a group of monks from a nearby monastery whose abbot had died. He reluctantly joined the abbey only to become the object of attempted murder; mysteriously escaping poison twice by what was apparently divine intervention. (16) And so began the legend of the many miracles attributed to Benedict. The influence of Benedict led one of his disciples to the papacy and to be later venerated as arguably one of the greatest popes that ever lived. (17) Gregory the Great (540-604) would come to lead the mutual admiration society for Saint Benedict, ultimately writing Benedict's biography with a zeal and conviction befitting a saint. The Rule of Saint Benedict remains the most influential in all monasteries.

Where the Augustinians and their derivatives may have served peripatetically, the rule of Saint Benedict required the monks and would-be postulants to sincerely promise stability. This was a serious commitment, to remain at one monastery for the rest of one's life. And yet many adherents would come to support the order and invariably the Roman Catholic Church. The monasteries would become bastions of stable and productive communities, with the abbot and his subordinate monks influencing education, farming, and local government functions—as well as promulgating religious dogma. With Rome as the principal authority, the Roman Catholic Church eventually came to wield profound influence throughout Europe and eventually in the far reaches of the other hemispheres, including the Americas. Certainly some resistance ensued and several factions of barbarians would eventually come to embrace Christianity and variations of induced civility. The steady and calculated dissemination of an inevitable belief system would not be deterred. One of the early pontiffs of the Catholic Church, Pope Leo the Great (400-61), made intrepid overtures to Attila the Hun and was able to successfully appease Attila and advance his standing among the pantheon of great bishops. (18) And this would have to be considered one of the harbingers of the travails and transition, as the demise of the Roman Empire gave way to the dark ages. What were once barbarians were now becoming the new royalty, feudal lords and minor kings in a world of upheaval—a world still tempered by the power of a belief.

In the establishment of the church, civilization and the complementary behavior must operate in tandem for the order of civility and the pursuit of one's faith to be sustainable, and most importantly real. With this insight Pope Gregory the Great set out to establish an advanced coenobitic civilization that would compensate for the inertia of the former Roman

Empire (that included loose alliances and a multiplicity of lingering enemies). Pope Gregory has been often described as the last of the four original Doctors of the Church, a lofty title of reverence to be sure; Gregory was also the driving force behind the pervasiveness of Benedictine monasticism. A skilled writer and administrator, Pope Gregory vigorously brought the papacy the grand prestige that transformed the Roman Catholic Church into the transcendent power that it ultimately became. Gregory made and kept peace with the invading Lombard contingent by paying annual bribes. This action suggests that throughout recorded history, some system of quid-pro-quo has existed between government powers and the "peaceful" existence of the church. These alliances between secular and spiritual realms tended to corrupt both parties and created chasms from without and from within the church. Gregory chose to ingratiate himself and pay tributes to promote peace while his master plan of disseminating Catholic religion took hold. History records that his plan worked to some degree, as the barbarian hordes of Lombards and Visigoths came to denounce Arianism and adopt Catholicism. (19)

The association and tenuous relationship between the papacy and the incipient polities of various power brokers developed a symbiosis that would come to be termed as Caesaropapism. In other words, the political establishment in power forced the subordination of the church and made its own religious claims to justify its policies/inclinations. Such an association would invariably lead to depravity for both entities in complex and often destructive ways. The true Christians in the church would have been torn with constant ambivalence relative to biblical teachings and the errant—contrary—posture of the church leader(s) and that of the king in a given locale. Pseudo-Christians and closet pagans would be oblivious to the deceit as long as their individual worlds were not impacted, especially if they were the recipient of bribery.

Pope Gregory I would be venerated by many and found deceitfully sinister from other perspectives. One theologian identifies a different Gregory the Great: a Pope that insidiously executed a master plan to place all earthly power in the hands of one man (the office of the papacy). John Dowling, in his seminal tome, paints a far less flattering picture of Gregory the Great and the office he is credited with consolidating at the turn of the seventh century. Pastor Dowling condemns Gregory as the man who not only established a corrupt papacy but would also contribute to innocent blood being spilled with his alliances for peace. (20) With cyclic certainty, the papacy would obtain and lose power through political intrigue for a number of centuries.

There would be one especially controversial pact that truly exemplified Caesaropapism (or perhaps more accurately Emperor-Pope) with the Carolingian Dynasty. Charles Martel was a take-no-prisoners type of autocrat that came to be known as "the Hammer." His son had some serious stones of his own (Pepin III), but it would be his grandson that would take center stage for the Europe of the last millennia. Charlemagne (742-814), would use the power of a belief and the force of his will to consolidate his empire through the coercive adoption of Christianity. This position would ultimately endear him to elements of the Roman Catholic Church and solidify his fame among some elite theologians, popes, and, as perhaps the last true emperor of the Roman Empire. The dichotomy of Charlemagne as a Germanic warrior on one hand and a friend of Roman Catholic Christianity on the other are subject to intense scrutiny. As Charles the Great he practiced horrific bloodletting in the name of espoused Christianity. The killing of God's children to force them into a "belief" has to be in opposition to any genuine monotheistic altruism as denoted in biblical teachings. Surely Charlemagne knew of the biblical sixth commandment and yet, on some level, his instincts and lineage caused him to take some pleasure in his sanguinary lust. He would have eventually killed his little brother Carloman (his co-ruler) if fate had not intervened with death visiting baby brother at the age of twenty. (21) Nevertheless, Charlemagne is historically afforded the benefit of composite truth, either by divine provenance or phenomenally good fortune as the time in question unfolded.

Charlemagne had been in war with his dad at the age of fifteen, and knew of a certain commitment his father had made to protect papal lands. The speculation is that Charles had an honest desire to honor his father and grandfather by supporting whatever the intentions relative to the church and its continued successful influence. No one knows for sure if Charlemagne's motives were of a certain virtue, or the mind-altering proclivity of absolute power. One thing is certain; Charlemagne distinguished himself in the annals of history by protecting a certain pope and ultimately allowing himself to be crowned Emperor of Rome on December 25th 800. The pontiff in this case was Pope Saint Leo III (750-816). This extraordinary coronation had been in the making for five years. Pope Leo III (795-816) was not the favorite son of Rome's aristocracy, and the antipathy that was projected at the pontiff became egregious, culminating with multiple charges that included adultery. Organized vigilantes conspired and ultimately they attacked the pope with murderous intentions, and nearly succeeded in gouging out Leo's eyes. (22) The pope was rescued by Magnus Forteman and a band of nobles. Deposed and confined to a monastery, Leo eventually escaped and traveled to meet Charlemagne. The Frankish king ordered his soldiers to neutralize all those that had conspired against Leo III. History records the assailants were purportedly ordered to one of Charlemagne's strongholds and eventually "dealt" with. (23) The gratitude, along with obligatory reciprocity, had to be an immense drive for the pontiff and after being restored to his rightful place in Rome, Pope Leo III crowned the supposedly unassuming Charlemagne Emperor of Rome. There are those that doubt the veracity of the claims that Charlemagne had no idea of what the pope intended and that the coronation was a complete surprise to him. Based on the previous insights on Caesaropapism, this version of history, pertaining to Charles the Great, is dubious at best. (24)

Charlemagne has been celebrated as the "King and Father of Europe" for his exploits in ultimately expanding Christianity and developing a social, political, and economic system that had lasting influence, long after the disintegration of the Carolingian Dynasty. (25) The political structure, and that of the ever-growing wave of Christianity (however diluted by religions of the dark ages), would continue to grow and become dominant through continual proliferation of the church and monastic paradigms. Monasticism developed schools of higher learning that were the first repositories of scholarly works which evolved to become libraries and universities. These institutions of higher learning, both temporal and spiritual, would greatly influence the communities that grew up around them. The brain trusts that also happened to be monks, priests, and abbots would invariably shape the local societal structure in any number of ways, some good and others subject to interpretation. Education would be limited to those associated with political power and that meant the Roman Catholic Church, on multiple levels.

The paradigm consistently worked because an examination of the modern-day universities reveals a high incidence of religious affiliation which includes the Roman Catholic Church. In the United States there are no less than 180 Catholic-based universities located in 39 of the 50 states, and that does not include preparatory schools. (26) Some Catholic universities boast of being the pinnacle of education, on the same level as the vaunted Ivy League schools. An elaborate internet web site is dedicated to the more highly publicized Catholic universities such as Boston College, Georgetown, Holy Cross, Notre Dame, and St John's, to name just a few. (27) Through the assiduous application of doctrine and dogma, eventually an ideology becomes not only accepted, but commonplace and natural. Such is the case with Roman Catholic influences in educating millions of fertile minds.

The Medieval era, for many years, was designated by brackets as early, high, and late Middle Ages. The early years were also referred to as the dark ages, with contemporary historians attempting to rename the period with a less negative connotation. The period from about 500 to 1000 would have to be as originally described: a very dark period when the major components of the era are fully acknowledged. There was the unsettling migration period of the Goths, Vandals, Huns, and other barbarians that lasted for centuries (400-700). (28) Superstition and broad-based ignorance was the norm. And the rise of Islam would challenge the belief system of those destined to shed blood for their own immutable Christian beliefs. The religion of Islam would pose a direct threat to the Roman Catholic Church and the continued dissemination of Catholicism to all corners of the earth. The struggle would yield prodigious bloodletting in multiple Crusades and peripheral battles as well. A myriad of vendettas continue into modern times; and although the actors, tactics, and technology have all changed, the power of a belief again dictates a certain insanity of reason. World civilization would decline through pandemic diseases of smallpox and the plague. Studies in history suggest an estimated 50 percent decline in the European population in the years 530 to 720. (29) Further analysis indicates decreased crop production (multiple theories as to why), partly attributed to barbarian conflicts and runaway slaves, hastened the destruction of the plantations. When we assimilate all of these factors in one cohesive tapestry, the Dark Ages is an apt description.

Inside the monastery, the darkness would be illuminated by the light of informed thought and deliberate reason in the context of spiritual enlightenment. Not all would shine so bright, but it appears that those of Italian descent and belonging to the Roman Catholic Church invariably found abundance and acclaim. A few exceptions would include Domingo Felix de Guzman, a Spanish preacher that would become Dominic. Saint Dominic (1170-1221), became the father of the Order of Dominicans, a religious order that would attempt to rival the Benedictines and yet eventually complement their senior counterparts under the auspices of the papacy in Rome. To accomplish this was no easy task; Dominic had to petition Pope Innocent III in person, finally achieving full sanction a year later by Pope Honorius III. (30) Catholicism has no boundaries and Spanish Catholics have the reverence required to live in the grace of the Holy Roman Empire and as an abiding extension of the Holy Father. Although there are distinct differences in the Benedictine and Dominican orders, Saint Dominic proved to Rome in so many words that a "preaching friar" could be an effective conveyance in disseminating Catholicism, even with slight variations. These differences could be effective in other parts of the world and among different people. And so the Dominicans came under the religious umbrella of the Roman Catholic Church and served the mandate of spreading Christ's word in conjunction with the Benedictine order. Although competition would have been forbidden, this discipline did not dissuade later priests from vigorously recruiting a future doctor of the Holy Roman Church. He was a devout holy man of formidable influence and utilitarian benevolence to the church.

Thomas Aquinas (1225-1274) appears to have been the reincarnation of Augustine in almost every way. Suffice to say that Thomas would have been more pure with respect to the ladies and carnal relations in general. His parents introduced him to religion at the age of five and were intent on his following in the footsteps of Benedict at the crown of monasteries, Monte Cassino. However, fate intervened and Thomas had to be moved to a safer monastery along with his parents' steadfast designs on his religious training and brand of monasticism. Evidently a precocious child, Thomas came to terms with his calling—identity—at an early age and chose to join the Dominican order as a teenager. His mother, Theodora, had a theological career path already planned for her son with the Benedictine order; and she held him against his will in an attempt to dissuade him from joining the Dominicans. The plan failed and Saint Dominic most likely smiled broadly in the grave with the coup his order had pulled off. In Thomas, the legend of his spirit affiliation with God may very well have been preordained, as his early mentor and Dominican scholar, Albertus Magnus, prognosticated when Saint Thomas was but 23 years old. (31) There are those that would rank Saint Thomas as the greatest of the medieval theologians; however, this writer believes that "the son cannot come before the father" and although Aquinas was great in amalgamation and articulation, he still stood on the shoulders of Aristotle, Averroes, Augustine of Hippo, and the influences of Albertus Magnus. A brilliant mind to be sure, it is Thomas Aquinas that greatly contributed to the evolution of monasticism into scholasticism, a discipline that became one of the dominant platforms of reason in succeeding centuries. The distinction of Thomas Aquinas lies in his writings and again the ability to articulate the realities of a mortal relationship with an omnipotent God. The human ability to use reason in deliberative thought is the apparent conduit or link between man and the Supreme Being. (32)

The Roman Catholic Church identified the greatness of Thomas Aquinas and through skillful adjudication, along with sedulous concentration, integrated biblical teachings with the theological philosophy of Saint Thomas. Of special note, the doctrine of biblical scripture and the established "tradition" of the Catholic Church are the reasons for such expansive latitude as the ultimate arbiter of Christianity. It is through this tradition that the Pope and the Roman Catholic Church are to be considered axiomatic in all matters of biblical understanding. (33) This was more than enough to make Thomas Aquinas one of the second-tier Doctors of the Church and ranking alongside St. Augustine and Gregory the Great. It could be said that in an evolving analysis, many aspects of modern philosophy were derived by subsequent thinkers both for and against the ideologies of Thomas Aquinas. (34)

In more recent times Protestant religious groups have taken exception to some of the Catholic Church's more controversial doctrines related to Apostolic Tradition. Some of these include the veneration of Mary, the confessional, indulgences, mortal sin, and purgatory, to name just a few. (35) This is not intended to maliciously malign the Catholic Church in any way; but it is an attempt to understand religious dogma, theology, and philosophy in the most truthful and unbiased exposure in the true spirit of philosophy (a lover of knowledge). Why the controversy? Where does worldwide passion, both for and against a religion, fit into the future viability of the planetary community? There are far more compelling questions relative to individual relations with one's God; but for the sake of civilization, none is more vital or crucial.

The military arms of the church deserve honorable mention in full disclosure and understanding. Monastic paradigms established and perpetuated by Roman Catholicism would come to sanction abbeys of military discipline and religious austerity. One of the foremost martial organizations sanctioned by the Roman Catholic Church was the Cistercian order. They were officially called to serve in the early twelfth century, with some historians claiming 1098 as the first year of named operations. (36) It would be 1100 before Pope Paschal II gave full sanction to the order and thus established a military division of operatives for the good of the church. Twenty years would pass before the "Poor Knights of Christ" would make their presence known protecting the pilgrims of Jerusalem. The Knights Templar became legendary for selfless dedication, and later for heresy and perhaps rivaling the first order so sanctioned by the Catholic Church. (37) The Templars had other competitors, such as the Hospitallers, whom they worked with and against in alternating quests for religious fame and monetary gain, with the church waiting in either event. The Cistercians were founded by a group of Benedictine monks in France; the Benedictine element alone gives greater credence for full sanction by the Pope and the Catholic Church. This is not to say that the other military orders did not serve the dictates of the church in one way or another. However, it is the contention of this writer that the Templars, Hospitallers, Dominican and Franciscan orders served various purposes for a time, and either grew uncontrollably corrupt (as was the case with the Templars) or simply outlived their usefulness. (38) Once the Templars became wealthy enough to start their own banking system, arrogance and depravity were an inevitable byproduct of near-absolute power and the sanctions of the papacy. (39)

The Hospitallers had been in existence since 1070 and yet their exploits were vastly overshadowed by the Templars and most assuredly by the Cistercian order. (40) The Cistercian order proved to be a disciplined and organized monastic force. The few challenges that tested the order early in its charter were rectified by the spiritual leadership of St. Bernard of Clairvaux, who joined the abbey in 1113. Bernard is credited with the successful expansion of the order, such that by 1150 there were over 300 monasteries extending throughout Europe and the British Isles. (41) The order eventually became loosely known by its constitution as the Charter of Charity. Rome and the papacy were evidently strong stalwart supporters of the order, far beyond the life cycle of the Knights Templar.

The politics of competing groups are such that the most flamboyant among those with the power, might become the target for elimination. This is apparently what happened to the Templars. Although history suggests that the Hospitallers were also being considered for retirement, they somehow made peace or "cut a deal" with the Holy See to prevent their prosecution ala the Templars. (42) The Hospitallers would go on to live prosperously on the Island of Rhodes for two centuries after the destruction of the Templars in 1312. And when adaptation was needed to survive incursions by the Ottoman Turks (1522), they simply became the Knights of Malta. The papacy gave its blessing to the order when the pope transferred some of the Templars' holdings over to the Hospitallers and most likely continued to benefit from the activities of the newly named Knights of Malta

Religious purists are naturally inclined to view the Dominican order with an idealized religious image. One historical theologian indicts Saint Dominic as being the first inquisitor-general of the holy inquisitions. The fiercely driven inquisition is purported to have included atrocious cruelty and specialized torture in the name of the Holy See. As the leader of the aggression in around 1207, Dominic was identified as sadistic, even bloodthirsty in sending numerous "heretics" to the gallows without mercy. Saint Francis of Assisi (1182-1226) is also branded as complicit in the bloodletting along with his Franciscan order. (43) Francis is known to have had trouble with dissention in his second order and left them to start his Third Order of Franciscans, also known as the tertiaries. This could have been precipitated by the legend of the mysterious stigmata afflicting Francis. In this brief overview we find that some of the most honored mendicant and monastic orders were not all paragons of virtue. However, they all had one thing in common: they each had the Roman Catholic Church as the principal sanctioning and controlling entity in all major aspects of the respective organizations.

The Knights Templar have for centuries been associated with a legend of vast treasure being hidden or otherwise used in the continued perpetuation of the group under a different identity. These myths related to lost treasure have been consistently infused with new blood in perennial generations. Unsubstantiated rumor and myth has been the subject of some notable searches for and claims of a vast Templar treasure. The "Money Pit" of Oak Island has elicited continuing intrigue and a number of books. (44) Logic and CSI type investigative techniques would tend to refute the theory of the Templars moving vast treasure across the Atlantic Ocean to store away in a complex booby trap in an unknown land, seemingly to never be unearthed again. Or maybe the legend of Templar treasure on Oak Island was an elaborate ruse to misdirect anyone inquiring about or pursuing the substantial wealth associated with the Templars. And let's not forget the Benedictine, Cistercian, Dominican, and Hospitallers orders would have made annual contributions to the Pope and the Roman Catholic Church. After the dissolution of the Templars, Pope Clement V gave some of the Templars' holdings to the other orders and most certainly a portion of those same possessions remained with the church.

The aspirations of The Holy Roman church would not be challenged by any earthly force. The three major Crusades are a testament to the resolve of the Catholic Church. An imperious nature is pervasive throughout all aspects of the Roman Catholic Church. For this reason, their base of supreme authority must complement and project the indomitable power of the Vicar of God. An edifice, known as St. Peter's Basilica, is the largest church in the world and the focal point of the Vatican in Rome. (45) The basilica of St. Peter's is emblematic of the pontificate and in literal terms, it is the universal church on this planet. As the largest church by volume and area, it commands the right as a world religious center. The monumental conception and will to build such a massive edifice required extraordinary commitment and money. A colossal church requires the equivalent planning, and by the middle of the 14th century the conception of said church would have been in place. With a huge bank account and the Templar treasure, along with perpetual income from the other Orders, the planning of the majestic basilica and ornate Vatican City would continue unimpeded until its unrivaled completion.

Beginning in 1503 under the auspices of Pope Julius II, Rome carefully yet assiduously began the construction of St. Peter's. It would take 176 years to complete with a progression of various architects and eminent artists that included Bramante, Michelangelo, and Raphael. (46) Other notable artisans by the likes of Bernini and Fontana contributed. In this scenario we have an estimated 350 years of planning, construction, and inexorable determination to make not only Catholicism eternal but also that of Rome. And so it is that such an edifice can command such exaltation. All one needs is to walk into the Basilica to know that beyond the granite and marble, a life force is infused in the aura and transcendental spirit that is Rome and the church as one.

The Renaissance was a time of progressive change and moral stagnation, all in one convincing stage play. As the art of language and the dictates of human self-expression increased, so too would the quest to understand the range of passion in human emotion and the accompanying introspection. Some might attribute these luminous progressions to increased education on multiple fronts. Scholasticism would now be in full character and the motives relative to the stage and evolving beliefs were now being disseminated through written word and theatrical expose`. Scholasticism now dominated philosophical discourse with relentless comparisons of the acknowledged authoritarians of the era. In the age of the Merchant, advancing trade and especially banking and credits would announce the philosophy of accessible money, power and prodigious appetites. Trade came to contribute to more material goods and philosophical ideologies being transferred and communicated across the world's hemispheres. These disseminating ideas would be adopted by some and challenged by others. Still other entities would take the desired tenets and alter or meld their own views into a new philosophy that could be embraced by a malleable culture.

Machiavelli, a name synonymous with cunning and treachery, may have accidentally instituted a deviant philosophy as the forerunner of political science. Niccolo Machiavelli (1469-1527), appears to have been an unassuming Italian in the wrong place at the right time to become famous for writing a book that was promoted posthumously after "Mack" had died a failure in his own mind. The corruption and quests for power of the time were as a revolving door in Italy and neighboring states as well. The period that tempered the philosophy of Machiavellianism has been adeptly assessed as a product of the treachery that Machiavelli was confronted with. (47) Some references in history would identify a man that simply wanted to be a part of the preservation of his beloved state and that he simply identified a systematic approach to managing the dictates of the politics of that time. (48) Self-preservation as well as respectable ambition drove Machiavelli to be sure, but it should be noted that he wrote *The Prince* after he had been first turned away and then severely tortured. He was subjected to the dreaded *strappado*, a torture technique that has the intent of ripping one's arms out of their sockets and causing various other internal injuries. (49) Disgraced and hurt, that is sure to make most any human spew vitriol. Did Machiavelli force us to confront what appears to be a maxim in human political psyche: that even a moral person must set aside ethics and morality in order to rule over a culture that has been conditioned (hard wired) for deceit and murder? (50) Fascinating how another Italian, born not far from Rome, has left an indelible influence on society worldwide, such that "political science" will dominate humanity until the last breaths are drawn.

Martin Luther, the man destined to repudiate the Roman Catholic Church and serve as the nexus in the quest for man to distinguish his relationship with God and biblical law. From the context of philosopher versus theologian, the strength to challenge Roman Catholic orthodoxy (and the papacy) required a mental—spiritual—conviction that would have had to anticipate the probable consequence of torture and death. Martin Luther personified a scholar's life, in the university and as an inquisitive mind. Scholasticism at that time would be at its zenith and this would have been the continuation from the monastic paradigm preceding the period. The Protestant Reformation is attributed to Luther, in many instances, without regard for some of the peripheral yet important factors leading to one of the most controversial and historically significant periods of early civilization. The document responsible for the chasm and subsequent religious controversy was the "Disputation of Martin Luther on the Power and Efficacy of Indulgences." This document came to be known as *The Ninety-Five Theses.* It profoundly rattled the Roman Catholic Church and its position as the absolute arbiter and gate keeper for interpreting the bible and the full understanding of the 'grace' of God. Luther reasoned that the written word of the bible did not sanction the sale of indulgences and that the pope was corrupt in perpetrating the extortion of money from God's people through erroneous religious justification. (51)

Surely there would have been other literate Christians capable of understanding the premise of God-given-grace by simply reading—studying—the bible as Luther had. Those same individuals evidently lacked the courage to speak about what was obviously contemplated by the same informed minds. An unbiased look at Martin Luther's motives indicates his original letter was written with piety and respect for the regional bishop, Albert of Mainz. There is evidence that some of Luther's friends took a copy of the *Theses* and converted it from Latin to German for further dissemination. This happened early in 1518, coinciding with the advancing use of the printing press. Johann Gutenberg had invented the sophisticated printing press in 1450. With prototypes perfected over 70 years, the power of the press hastened the broad distribution of Martin Luther's life-altering and religiously liberating truth—which was zealously embraced. The paper was aggressively copied and within weeks had spread all over Germany and within a few months the rest of Europe as well. It is accurate to say that the printing press contributed to the controversy taking on a life of its own, similar to modern-day press sensationalism. (52)

The German people had for centuries been subjugated by the empire of Rome in one form or another. The era of the Caesars had given way to the Holy Roman Church and the papacy. With Luther as their champion, the Teutonic people now had a new more comfortable religion to embrace and happily shed the yoke of Rome—in one decisive blow. The new religion of Lutheranism spread far and wide and even spawned splinter groups with variations of the Lutheran church. Martin Luther, an ordained priest since the age of 24, was now an enemy of the Roman Catholic Church. He was brought up on charges of heresy, condemned as a criminal and by some accounts, "wanted dead or alive." However, the more Luther was attacked, the more rampant the institution of the Lutheran faith became. Pope Leo X first warned Luther and then excoriated him; ultimately the pope excommunicated Luther in 1521. To insulate the pontificate, "secular authorities" were unleashed on Luther. With the help of friends, Martin Luther either escaped or was shielded from harm by a circle of confidants and a formidable throng of parishioners. Luther set a new ideal in place of the outwardly restrictive rules that governed the Roman Catholic hierarchy. Martin Luther wrote extensively, established the new church, produced hymns, encouraged human interaction in the mass, and most importantly allowed for the priests to marry and have some semblance of a normal life.

The life of Martin Luther was not without personal controversy, even beyond his conflict with the Catholic Church. Although he appears to have chosen wisely in his marriage to a former Cistercian Nun (Katharina), three of his six children died tragically before reaching adulthood. He became embroiled in a scandal that suggested Luther was a hypocrite as to the sanctity of marriage—not his but that of Philip of Hesse. Phillip solicited advice from the theologian and Luther apparently advised the soon-to-be bigamist to quietly marry the paramour (against tradition) and in addition to his current wife. The secret did not stay secret for long, and Luther was implicated and thoroughly denounced for his part in the disgraceful affair. This indiscretion would haunt Martin Luther for the rest of his life.

Martin Luther was also purported to dislike Jews and this was the focus of some of his writings that were identified as anti-Semitic. In one of his final books, published in 1543 and just three years before his death, Luther took an extremely divisive tone against those of Jewish origin. This position is extremely contrary to the established history of Martin Luther with respect to the profound insights that he displayed with aspects of biblical understanding previously presented. Surely Luther would be familiar with 1 John 4: 7-8, and the same book acutely denounces the position of mortal judgment that Luther disseminated. (53) In the liberation from one religion for another, people died and many swore vengeance. The peasant wars could be, at least indirectly, attributed to Martin Luther and although he spoke against the radicalism in the years 1524-25, there was widespread bloodshed in Luther's name. All of the carnage cannot be totally attributed to Luther or his message; the papacy and Rome had a hand in exacerbating a divergent runaway human quest for religious truth.

The fact that Henry VIII chose to break with Rome during this time period (Anne Boleyn and lust notwithstanding) suggests Luther's Reformation may have emboldened the English monarch. And with this, the subsequent formation of the English Church further weakened the papacy and the Roman Catholic Church. The aggressive opposition instituted by Rome greatly contributed to the Protestant Reformation in that—an individual relationship with God must be chosen of free will and uncorrupted by an intercessor such as the pope.

Opposition to the Roman Catholic Church may very well have been preordained. The time and the manifestation of the conflict remain predicated on the first established church in recorded history. This formulated a position or thesis that, in accordance with another descendent of Teutonic blood-line, could only cause an opposing position or the antithesis of, in this case, the Roman Catholic Church. For several centuries the Roman church controlled, neutralized, or killed all opposing religious beliefs. The church would evolve and improve on the monastic and scholastic systems with operatives like that of the Jesuit Order (1534). And the Counter Reformation could be easily identified as the next thesis to oppose the Protestant Reformation. This calls to mind the inevitability of division, opposition and again the power of a belief.

Georg W. F. Hegel (1770-1831) was one to identify, perhaps through the reformation, his philosophy of dialectic thinking. Born in Germany two centuries after Luther, but a product of Lutheranism nonetheless, Hegel reasoned that there must always be a counter point in all advances in reasoning, philosophy and inevitably religion as well. This idealism is intended to promote advances in human culture to the highest evolutionary intellect.

The advanced logic that Hegel espoused, although complex in the abstract, is efficacious if skillfully and tactfully executed. Beginning with the basics: the *thesis* is the first position or dictate, usually considered incomplete, to begin or set in motion a counter point or *antithesis* that is formulated in opposition to the original thesis. Through the inevitable conflict, machinations that may include extended debate, protracted battles, bribery, Machiavellianism, and a host of other influences are designed to bring the original idea closer to the intended *synthesis*. This invariably creates another polemic that provokes opposition and the cycle continues for as long as there is energy to sustain the conflict. (54) That energy may come from or through a puppet master that can sustain the conflict to his or her designed end. Hegel, on some level, may have discovered a character trait in the natural evolutionary process of a civilized society that is captive to human vice, politics, greed, and passion. That aspect of human proclivity to calculate, conspire, and manipulate for one's own ends are part and parcel to human existence in both religious and philosophic realms.

The conflict initiated by the two reformations (Protestant and Counter) is a classic example of Hegelian principle. The Catholic Church tried to quell Luther by attacking him even after the light of an open bible had exposed the depravity of the then-papacy. After realizing that fabricated character assassination could not stop a fervent opponent, they simply created another thesis. Hegelian principles have been adapted in political science and are in constant use in almost all aspects of civilized society. In the United States, a two-party political system (Democrat versus Republican) forms the first two parts of the triad. Decade after decade one party will rule over the American people and then the other with divisively polarizing legislation and mandates constantly creating ever more synthesis to begin the process yet again. The evolution of religious controversy reveals the Roman Catholic Church insinuating its influence into other religious denominations; the Methodist Church is one example. (If we cannot be the only church we will formulate the plan to somehow be in all church religion).

With the religion or thesis, we can now view philosophy as the antithesis and the comingling as the synthesis. Not so fast, did we not speak to this back in the last centuries of the Roman Empire? Well, yes but the full knowledge of a continuously evolving civilization forces us to face the lack of complete insight into not only human identity, but the full understanding of what we can grasp as real in a given construct. In Hegelian philosophy, the "ideal" or absolute reality can only be achieved by the constant ascendency of the dialectic. (55) If Hegel is right (and only the whole constitutes truth) then we as a species will always be in shifting sand and chasing shadows in a quest to find what can never be attained. (An analogy would be comparable to a human being attempting to approach the speed of light using conventional physics). And for some that is just fine with them, because by the time a formidable contingent figures out what happened, the perpetrators are so far removed from the deed that accountability for the transgression will be nearly impossible. And the suspects, most likely, will have all died.

It could be said that the Wall Street bankers of 2008 used Hegelian principle to fleece the American populace out of billions of dollars. They first created a special banking **thesis** that was years in the making with the changing of banking laws (Glass-Steagall Act) and through the purchase of politicians. (56) Then, by setting the stage to embezzle the wealth of the U.S. population through the illusion of prosperity and home ownership, they rigged the economy to fail with derivative and leveraged banking mechanisms or the **antithesis**. The contrived economic downturn forced the middleclass to pay—through taxes—for the new emperors and minor kings that ultimately profited (**synthesis**) from their conspiracy to defraud the common people of their life energy and meager share of the earth's bounty. The reality of what happened during the worldwide financial crises of 2008-2010 is easily juxtaposed with Hegelian philosophic principles; all one needs to do is perform an analysis of all the particulars to understand the evolved *Dialectic* as true, at its Hegelian best.

Immanuel Kant (1724-1804), one of the principal German philosophers that preceded Hegel and definitely influenced the dialectic author with some original thoughts of his own. Kant is widely held as one the most influential thinkers of the enlightenment era. His contribution to philosophy is multi-faceted and equally complex when compared to his successor(s). Kant distinguished his perceptions in what would be termed empirical knowledge, and decisively acknowledged a spiritual reality he termed as the *noumenal*. Empirically was—is where we humans live, and based on *phenomenal*, that is all we can ever be sure of—and even that is fleeting. Things, as they appear, are constantly subject to human interpretation according to Kant. And here lies the challenge: because of the inherent human filters and mechanism of perception, we greatly influence our experiences and perceptions from within an unknown reality! If each one of us creates our own reality, even with basic human conventions in agreement, we are still unsure—beyond accepted convention—of what is truly real. For example, we all have had vivid dreams or nightmares that seemed indistinguishable from a "real" and waking experience. Our brain process for accessing a pleasurable memory is very similar to recalling a dream; the similarity is cause for heuristic inquiry into our known (accepted) reality.

Kant appears to have come to a certain agreement with Plato on the premise of innate knowledge. He referred to it as the *priori* and that the intuitions we use are necessary to help formulate a coherent reference for understanding all of the earthly sensory inputs that confront human existence. Kant was also somewhat contradictory in the full range of his philosophy. He was concerned with moral issues that were predicated on an individual's duty, sometimes referred to as deontological ethics. This philosophy rigidly adheres to doing the right thing and being of sound moral motivation as well. In other words you need to comport yourself in a civil society based solely on lawful convention and a morally directed conscience. This would conflict with certain virtue ethics, where someone broke the law to save another person's life and the ends were justified by the means by virtue of a positive outcome. This is also known as teleological ethics, whereby the positive outcome determines whether the act is good or evil. The slippery slope comes in the interpretation of what the true nature of good or evil was with respect to the participant(s) and their intent at the time.

Kant, along with Hegel, had a few flaws that call into question how astute they were in totality. Scholars of Kant and Hegel identify men that were intensely racist in erroneously classifying Blacks and Chinese as inferior beings. According to Kant, these inferior people were not capable of the intellectual aptitude of the "white skin" people, and the American Indian was even lower on Kant's intelligence scale so designated at the time. (57) Apparently Kant and Hegel failed to acknowledge certain truths pertaining to the existence of people slightly different from themselves. Regardless of what color or physical attributes a race of people may possess, the particular race had no choice in the matter. The white man, on an individual basis or otherwise, could not have "special ordered blond hair and blue eyes" preceding conception and in the womb. And the same truth is inherent in all races as well. We are all born, learn as we grow, and are modeled to accept our respective station and adapt accordingly; these truths evidently escaped certain philosophers. There were sexist attitudes that failed to acknowledge the intellect of women, and some writings would be considered misogynistic. These revered philosophers were not infallible; moreover they may have misdirected society down a degenerate path when all of the particulars are considered. How many sound and insightful minds were restricted (impeded) by bigotry and bias? Kant may have actually thought that innate—all—knowledge was governed by the amount of melanin in the skin.

The more useful insights that Kant espoused have some legitimate merit when analyzed in the context of modern civilization. In understanding the ideology that deontological ethics serve a very real and important purpose: If lying, for example, were to become an ordinary and accepted human convention, our system of communication and normal reality would degenerate into perpetual chaos...madness. (58) It is quite possible that the espoused innate knowledge would naturally guide most of humanity in the collective quest to survive. It stands to reason that the philosophies of Gnosticism, empiricism, relativism, and a host of other isms, appear to be the tangible derivatives of the various human belief systems in the personal search for an alternative power. Philosophy provides comfort through a mental construct for the atheists and agnostics that remain unconvinced within the shadows of their own composite reality. Kant evidently theorized that the latent influences of the late Roman Empire helped mold the thought processes of reason for most of the succeeding philosophers.

Francis Bacon (1561-1626) considered by many to be the catalyst for the fervor in empirical thought in the early years of the enlightenment. (59) Bacon may have been more statesman than philosopher; however, his affinity for scientific empirical pursuits may have contributed to his early death. His contributions to the scientific method extend into modern science theory. Controversially, his recurring association with some of the works of William Shakespeare must have some basis in truth if only through the indirect influences of Queen Elizabeth I and her court. Bacon was born 3 years before Shakespeare and lived on a full decade longer. It should also be noted that the exact dates of some of Shakespeare's works remain a mystery. The means and opportunity exists, however motive may be lacking. A wily politician would be more dangerous than a romantic dramatist and more likely to use such cunning for ulterior motives.

Rene` Descartes (1596-1650) the author of Cartesian philosophy, or **doubt** if you prefer. The idea of separating thought from existence is novel from a certain perspective; but Descartes was better at mathematics and that's where the story should end for him. I think and so I exist (more accurately, "I think therefore I am") or so the "profound" words announce the claim to fame. Two of our original wise men beat Descartes to the grail, and they even allowed us to maintain relative sanity at no additional cost. This insight, or alternative philosophy, opened the door for *solipsism*, a perilous mind practice in which we could feasibly make aspects of reality unreal. If all you can be sure of is yourself, then all social ties and interrelated acts could become extinct. For example, if no one believed in a material object, conceived and constructed by human hands, then that object would cease to exist. If no one believed in the telephone held in his or her hand it would have to vanish into oblivion. Remember, a telephone had to be conceived in someone's mind before becoming reality. This may seem facile but it is much more complex than most realize. If the mind can conceive of an object then surely the same mind can make it disappear, fade away, or not exist. Thought provocateurs like **Edmund Husserl** pushed Descartes' reasoning into an alternate philosophical realm using similar concepts. Idealism brings us yet closer to the amalgam of the civilized society. Through such processes we are able to continuously reinvent a given reality, as long as there is sufficient energy and the vast majority continue to believe in and push ever forward in the spirit of an idealized existence.

John Locke (1632-1704), the British philosopher renowned for his predilection for empiricism, contributed to the structure of the American constitution through his support for personal freedom and property rights. Imagine an Englishman contributing to the eventual establishment of American independence from the crown of England, ironic and apropos with all points in focus. Locke's pronouncement that natural law endowed humans, all humans, with certain inalienable rights personified the universal acceptance of humanity. The movement associated with utilitarianism brings us closer to the grand materialism that makes capitalism what it is today. In order to do the most good for the most number of people, there had to be vast production models to satisfy the "needs" and desires of the growing interlinked societies that were burgeoning in the eighteenth century. **Jeremy Bentham** (1748-1832), perhaps driven by hedonism in its purest form, is credited with the introduction of utilitarianism. Bentham could only see pain or pleasure in his understanding of human drives and was evidently influenced by Epicurus, the original high-priest of hedonism. In the first liberal foundations of social accommodation, philosophic views "morphed" to become an alternative religion through social contracts, laws, property rights, and the strata of aristocracy.

John Stuart Mill would follow his father, James Mill, (a top student of Bentham) and expand the principles set forth by Bentham in a variation of utilitarianism that included political science. A true trailblazer for the times, J.S. Mill (1806-1873), advocated not only property rights but equal rights for women—contributing to the suffrage movement of the mid-nineteenth century. This was very radical for the times and eccentric for even advanced thinkers like Mill. Through the incremental growth in reason (philosophy), history indicates rationale spawned the new religion of "self" versus the changeable questions of human association with the Supreme Being. What could man create in his newfound industrial world of more production, distribution, desire, and the right to pursue happiness at any cost? As no one was technically hurt and the practice of my "religion" satisfied that part of human nature, well… It could be said that through the comingling and evolution of the various philosophical systems, the most influential has been that of utilitarianism. (60) With the United States as the prototypical exemplification through economics and politics, utilitarianism is manifested in the social dynamic by less human suffering. (And if necessary, we will develop new laws in pursuit of this ideal).

The religion of self altered certain perspectives relative to ingrained moral inclinations. Our proclivities, comparable to what was right and what was truth, continuously evolve and change in much the same way the great minds alluded to in layered and exhaustive treatises. If nothing physically stays the same, and that powerful entity we call our mind is in a constant state of flux, then why bother with convention, outmoded morals, or restrictive laws? **Soren Kierkegaard** (1813-1855) left a profound influence on philosophy and in fact the world. Although he died before the evolved fruition of his thoughts became revered in the philosophic realm, **existentialism** is attributed to him posthumously and without question. (61) Our lives are nothing but dread, or so it was for Soren Kierkegaard. We can never be sure of anything, so, why should we care about the choices that we make? Just do whatever brings you your own individual existence. Live for the moment, do not try to understand; live before you die. This approach to life can be very liberating. No need to believe in or care about anything—beyond one's own death. These attitudes and eventual norms would be endorsed and promoted by ardent followers of the philosophy which included **Martin Heidegger** and **Jean-Paul Sartre** (1905-1980). In fairness to Kierkegaard, Sartre and Heidegger were both atheists and Soren still held out some belief in God, even if from an otherwise quasi-deist perspective.

The modern-day philosophers that espouse existentialism are the products of college professors and academia from the twentieth century. Sartre has been mentioned, but he most assuredly influenced his band of followers who went on to disseminate similar teachings to their students. Recall that philosophy, especially one which is advocated by a pedagogue, has the power to alter social consciousness. Existentialism has subtly influenced some of the innate morality of society and contributed to the systemic apostasy that has become pervasive in the United States. (62) This dilution of faith is not confined to the anonymous pedestrian. The clergy, actual theologians, have seemingly lost conviction in many basic moral and biblical teachings—exemplified by one priest urging his congregation to steal if necessary. (63) The philosophy of the established churches has justified allowing dramatic changes in their hierarchy and in the commitment to faith intended to worship God instead of self. (64)

The graduated test for the sliding scale of truth relentlessly challenges the civilized conventions that are intended to make the varying philosophies and religions function in a given society. When these composite truths violently conflict, then the inevitable breakdown of society begins. Even in the court systems of democracies around the world, the judges that were chosen or elected to interpret law have succumbed to their own respective religions and have become "activist" judges. The ardor of the power bestowed upon these judges allows them to legislate from the bench, in effect making law—instead of interpreting the law as the office of judge was intended. The time frame indicates a great number of judges, in the United States and abroad, was influenced by existentialism based on some of the pronouncements that have come from the court system over the last forty years.

The courts and variable truths are easily connected to the rise of the plutocracy. The wealthy would have the world believe it is essential to have the lion's share of earthly bounty be secured in the hands of a few. It is interesting to note how one New York billionaire was not only able to change the laws related to term limits for the mayoral election, he essentially purchased the office of mayor with his vast fortune. (65) Other would-be public servants (many multi-millionaires and billionaires) have run campaigns strictly on personal monetary appeal. Why would a billionaire want to be elected to the office of governor, a job that only pays a fraction of the interest money that a billionaire receives weekly? (66) Sure, there are other notable motivations for a prodigiously rich plutocrat that has aspirations of holding public office and making the world a better place for all....

And then there are the entrenched career politicians that will defend the office at all costs and without shame or reservation. Millions, even billions, of dollars are spent on campaigns that are no more than hobbies for some politicians. We must acknowledge the elaborate corruption and subterfuge—masquerading as lobbyists or a political action committee in diplomatic parlance. The lobby, another name for legalized bribery, controls the elected officials that swore an oath to support and defend the constitution of the United States. Once the newly elected politician enters the Washington D.C. arena, their ability to resist corruption fades like last evening's sunset. (67) The list is endless and the reader will find his own special example to ruminate or fulminate over in his or her custom standard.

(68) The rampant depravity among the elect has contributed to most of America distrusting the government on almost all levels. (69) The structure of modern society allows flawed mortals (also known as elected officials) to sometimes make ruinous decisions that are based on philosophies and religions that have origins from the latent and transcendental influences of the Roman Empire.

Beginning with Rome and inclusive of the time of Socrates, Plato, and Aristotle, the foundations of an evolving philosophic construct and natural-rights allowed a multiplicity of beliefs to forge our modern civilization. The evolution of thought and reason brought humanity both closer to a belief in a Supreme Being and provoked antipathy for such a concept in a capricious and futile human existence. Pain and suffering from a benevolent God; how could that be? A mental and sometime spiritual ideal—shared by a social collective—had a universal appeal that offered the promise of comfort if only for an ephemeral episode. The cyclic nature of our temporal existence brought new blood, ideas, and philosophies of which to counteract fear, doubt, and inequity. The thesis of an omnipotent and jealous God, who commanded those with the strength to believe, forms a period of prevalence that ultimately creates a critical mass and the ensuing antithesis. Conflicting views and belief systems inexorably lead to an evolving synthesis that placates the majority for a cycle of time, but invariably sparks the fire of the next great empire.

Roman Rule(s)

In the annals of archaeology the Roman Empire stands alone as the focal point for all comparative analysis among relevant historical civilizations. The Egyptians, for example, may have left some thought-provoking monuments and phenomenal treasure, but with that culture's preoccupation with death it becomes easy to chart a graveyard and the associated implications. The Roman Empire was focused, even transfixed, on life, and especially growth; this is what makes the study of the Roman Imperial life-cycle far more compelling. The adoption of many of the late empire's command and governmental structures by the United States speaks to the quest of emulating the majesty of one of the most revered and enigmatic empires. Many of the same parallels that America and the Roman Empire share are indicative of the mystical relationship that exists on multiple levels. Many have come before to make comparisons, but in this exposition I sought to focus on the peripheral nuances of imitation and the latent bonds that give credence to the rationale. Various aspects of American culture are derivative of Roman ancestry and are ingrained in the hybrid identity of Americana.

Reincarnated through an incipient country of immigrants, the English, French, Italian, German, Spanish and various others may have seemed barbaric (new barbarians, if you prefer) to the indigenous Indians of the original continent now known as America. The relentless search for riches, philosophic and religious freedom, or simple conquest is reminiscent of an eternal fire that burns in Rome as in its descendents. What is identified as the compilation of multiple cultures and variations of themes cannot preclude the obvious and unrelenting spirit of the Roman Empire. In predestination we find our progenitors dividing antiquity between B.C.

and A.D. while standing watch at the birth of Christ and the Nova of not only Christianity but all interrelated world views.

It is doubtful that many knew the miraculous phenomenon known as the birth of Christ, would influence all succeeding cultures throughout the world. And then a scant 33 years later, the spectacle of a historic crucifixion was sanctioned and executed by the Roman powers of the world. Tiberius, Roman Emperor from 14-37 A.D., escaped culpability in that his appointed Roman governor in that region sent the distinguished Messiah named Jesus to his death by crucifixion on a cross. Several allegorical interpretations of the spectacle have survived and morphed into intriguing legends that support profound implications related to the Messiah. Prophesies abound, along with the spectacles and preternatural occurrences that support the preeminence of Christianity. A Roman centurion, during the final moments of the crucifixion, impaled the nearly dead or already late Messiah with a spear in his side and initiated a unique facet of supernatural intrigue.

The blood from Jesus Christ is purported to have imbued the soldier's lance with supernatural powers, such that anyone who dared to possess the spear would be invincible. However the manifestation of the spear's power came to be known, it incited the intense desire of several historical figures for two millennia. Religious leaders of the Roman Catholic Church aggressively sought possession of the spear for the mere association with Jesus Christ. There are four spears of unequal renown that command world attention. One resides in Rome and is most assuredly the "genuine article" among the espoused examples. (1) Another is the property of the Hapsburg Treasure House Museum in Vienna, Austria—the same one that drove Adolph Hitler nearly insane in his quest to possess it. Known as the Spear of Destiny, Hitler is purported to have studied the spear and the legend for 25 years, making it an obsession that climaxed in 1938 when he marched into Vienna and took possession of the mystical lance. A little more than one year later, Adolph Hitler attacked Poland and announced the beginning of World War II.

The legend of the spear alleged that anyone who possessed the lance would rule the world, and Hitler believed in and took that legend to a notable extreme. An interesting corollary to the story is revealed late in WWII, as the American army invaded Nuremberg, Germany and brought an end to Adolph Hitler on April 30, 1945. American military officials took possession of the spear and shortly thereafter the United States dropped the first atomic bomb on Japan, ultimately ending the war and essentially becoming the absolute ruler of the world, exactly as the legend of the spear had proclaimed. (2)

The prophecy of the spear is revealed in John 19: 31-37. In simple terms the stabbing of Jesus on the cross and, by inference, the power of the lance was foretold—with Rome again intimately involved. The soldier that stabbed the crucified Jesus is the same man that uttered the words proclaiming him as the true Messiah with profound awe and guilt. That centurion, Longinus, would eventually be forgiven and venerated as a saint by the Roman Catholic Church. (3) In this tale of preordained death, reverence, and forgiveness it is the rule of Rome that plays an integral part in all facets of the prophecy. This continues into modern times with those in control of "the spear." An added association, through the smearing of the blood from "the spear" to another spear, has given the power to at least two spears, one in Rome at the Vatican and the other in Vienna. It is the Viennese lance that was held by the United States during the successful detonation of the atomic bomb, the most powerful mechanized weapon the world had seen up until that point in history. After the war the spear was returned to its original and presumably proper resting place. The origins of the spear of destiny began with Rome, but ultimately the heir to the continuing empire, the United States, was seemingly endowed with the power of the spear for a predetermined appointment with destiny.

In the chronicles of history the copious myths and legends related to the Spear of Destiny have been analyzed as somewhat contradictory. If the holder of the true lance rules the world, then how is the U.S. the lone world superpower without actually possessing the lance? (4) It is not necessary for the United States to actually physically hold the spear, as long as the intended beneficiaries are taken care of. The Holy Roman Empire gave credence to the spear for over 1000 years, with Charlemagne claiming its power to be the reason for his success in all of his major victories. (5) Even Constantine the Great attributed some of his achievements and fortune to the spear. In Vienna, the Habsburg Monarchy, reigning from 1278-1780, staked a claim to the spear and a holy blood-line that was heavily associated with the Holy Roman Empire. One way or another, the spear's power, and its preternatural influences, were to belong to Rome. (6)

All roads led to Rome for the purpose of domination through the taxation of commerce, travel and control. Rome may have been situated on the long peninsula known as Italy, but the tentacles of the far flung empire directed all towards the center of the world. The Appian Way was so well constructed that 2000 years later, modern vehicles now traverse its overlaid cobblestones, a true testament to Roman construction and the enduring legacy left for its progeny to copy. The 53,000 miles of Roman roads still extant have been emulated by the United States interstate highway system that was begun in the 1950s and completed in the late 1980s. The highway system in the United States is the finest in the world in terms of convenience, size, and ubiquity across the contiguous continent. Some of the same road building techniques used by the Roman engineers have been adopted and utilized in United States road construction. (7) The layered bed of three to four feet thick and varying rock aggregates were good enough for the Romans and the same road building technique has worked well in the U.S. The testament is in the numbers: in 2010 Americans drove just over 3 trillion miles, matching the high mileage marks of 2006 and 2007. (8) It seems the father of empires knew something about the power of roads, and this is reflected in the love affair Americans have with their cars. With over 200 million functioning cars in the U. S. (2010), the automobile is an industry, institution, and revenue-generating platform without equal.

In Chapter Three, the automobile was highly profiled by the use of petroleum. That is but one component of the income generated by the exploitation of the internal combustion engine. Our economic calculations of automobile and road use must be assessed in the full spectrum of total revenue generation. There may be a toll booth in the area somewhere near you and awaiting payment for the use of your favorite corridor. Those taxes (also known as tolls) combined with motor fuel taxes, along with special tire purchase and disposal fees, can make a state budget comptroller's year in many respects. Our evolution in travel and the associated economic effect are important to all citizens and even more important to the Emperor— our President.

The second largest state in the U.S. is where vast amounts of fuel are produced, distributed, and linked throughout the North American continent. Besides fuel production Texas serves as the major gateway for trade with Mexico. With the North American Free Trade Agreement (NAFTA) Texas plays a key role in the shipment of oil, manufacturing, and low-cost imported goods from China and Mexico through what has become known as the Trans-Texas Corridor (TTC). The TTC was originally intended to be built and paid for by Americans to provide a direct and special money generator for Spain, a member of the European Union (EU). Although the initiative was "officially" defeated by outraged Texas citizens, unofficially the sinister plan has been repackaged and is being implemented using stealth tactics. The new plan calls for using the existing U.S. interstate highway system already in place and the Spanish company Cintra collecting the toll money. (9) Texas government officials are only too happy to sign a contract with a foreign government consortium (Cintra-Zachry) to control American infrastructure already paid for and belonging to America. The myriad of controversies include the arbitrary confiscation of private property, revised eminent domain laws, and a foreign country profiting off of the "life energy" of sovereign United States citizens. (10) This is only one component of the plan to integrate Canada, Mexico, and the United States into one trading block renamed the North American Union (NAU). This would be in addition to and in conjunction with the European Union. (11)

Texas is not the only U.S. state that is ready to sell out the America people to foreign interlopers. Pennsylvania has purportedly attempted to sell the Pennsylvania turnpike to Middle Eastern Arabs for a few billion dollars. (12) In places like northern Indiana and the Chicago Skyway, foreign entities lease the rights to collect tolls on roadways for extended periods of time. Technical ownership may very well be in the hands of member states of the European Union via proxy consortiums like Cintra-Zachry. (13) With massive state deficits across the United States, some of the states such as California, Minnesota, and Illinois are ready to take drastic steps to avert a fiscal default. California, the eighth largest economy in the world, has been downgraded in credit rating to A- status—the bottom of the list for the 50 states. (14) Dire straits make state governments susceptible to stop-gap measures that could be deemed less than prudent and even unethical.

The wheel has brought tremendous wealth to the U.S.; it has also brought incomparable wealth to oil-producing Arabian countries. So much wealth resides in the hands of the oil cartels that they have had to develop special banking money pools known as Sovereign Wealth Funds. These SWF funds are so vast that they enable the owners to literally buy countries, albeit a piece at a time. As strange as the concept may read, the United States may very well have provided such phenomenal wealth to the Arabs through oil consumption, that they (the Arabs) may be able to institute a new Monarchy, with the United States as a colonial holding. The hybrid repositories of wealth aforementioned could in fact be jointly controlled by unknown foreign entities that invested with the Arabs in elaborate collusion. Their ulterior motives are to ultimately subvert the United States through our country's addiction to foreign oil. This is not fiction; a historic review of the 1973 Arab oil embargo, and the peripheral effects, explains many of the nuances pertaining to the last four decades of oil consumption, money generation, and oil as a geopolitical weapon. The United States' association with Israel is a powerful inducement in the annals of senseless hatred perpetrated by Arabs and their oil cartels. (15)

Islamic hatred of Israel, and anyone that helps Israel, is historically chronicled over many centuries. In modern times much of the Islamic animosity is based on the nuclear weapons issue; Israel has nukes and its neighbors are prohibited from joining the club. Perceived instability and Islamic radicalism are the primary reasons cited in United States and NATO policy for withholding nuclear arms from countries like Iran, Iraq, and other hard-core Islamic nations. (16) The historic violence associated with Islam has considerable merit when judged throughout known precedent. *"First, the argument is made that Islam has from the start been a religion of the sword and that it glorifies military virtues. Islam originated among "warring Bedouin nomadic tribes" and this "violent origin is stamped in the foundation of Islam." Muhammad himself is remembered as a hard fighter and a skillful military commander."* (17) Terrorism and its close relative, guerilla warfare, can be extremely effective when strategically executed. However, the new warfare of money control will be the modern battleground providing an especially adept control of the masses, owing to the fact that American success, its culture, and economy are inextricably ensnared by the automobile and the concomitant use of roads, and thusly the toll. Consumers will pay the toll in one way or the other, as even those that do not drive must pay for sustenance and other consumables that are delivered across the country by trucks.

As an autonomously free society we are still captive to the energy infrastructure instituted by the titans of capitalism from the late nineteenth century. Their descendants refuse to allow any other reasonable competing alternatives to enter the arena and thusly remain the monopolistic oppressor's intent on dominating the world. These ultra-rich men and women of the earth, many associated with oil or related enterprises, are in contention to be the first trillionaire. European Union is in fact the revised Roman Empire with a new name and modus operandi. In order to institute an empire, conspiracy is essential in planning, execution, and the successful accomplishment with the least amount of collateral damage. Just as a bloodless coup is preferable to protracted battles, so too, is commandeering a country's wealth and superpower status while said country actually believes it is still in power. When the United States agreed to submit its sovereignty to the United Nations and pay the largest share of the operating expenses, it effectively nicked an artery that has been bleeding for over half a century. The same can be said of the United States accepting the world policing duties and suffering the largest loss of human life and unbalanced share of wasted bloodshed. Meanwhile, European countries (EU) have benefited by focusing on developing their infrastructure, economies, and world financial power. This will serve the conspiracy by the European Union in eviscerating the United States by using stealth tactics that are hybrid geopolitical warfare. By allowing the U.S. to bear most of the burdens, the European Union is exploiting United States innovation, productivity and wealth through dubious, unbalanced treaties such as GATT and WTO. The ultimate intention is the confiscation of U.S. assets and the eventual subjugation of America. The new emperor is the same as the old emperor with respect to the motives of conquest through confiscatory appropriation, a method perfected by the late Roman Empire.

The formidable tax revenue stream generated by the United States populace has been coveted by members of the E.U. for many decades. Great Britain has profited nicely from the coffers of the U.S., in one form or another. The phenomenal wealth generated by the American people has led to the unbridled looting of the treasury by politicians, Wall Street crooks, and investors in and of the U.S. military-industrial complex. It is the incessant theft, through perceived legitimacy and outright graft that has brought the U.S. to near fiscal insolvency. I write "near" because of the unmatched productivity and proclivity of America to create new and prolific business models and technological inventions that set the United State apart from most other countries—on the level of three-dimensional chess.

Perceived insolvency by some countries, such as China, has brought into question the future financial stability of the United States. Moreover, the Arabian oil cartels have sparked a cacophony of vociferous calls for a new world reserve currency and the condemnation of American dollars. (18) The very countries that earned the most from U.S. oil consumption are now conspiring to use financial brinksmanship to weaken the United States and set the stage for the final conquest. China, a country that has profited handsomely from U.S. consumption of their products, is aggressively criticizing the U.S. while it plots to secure oil supplies and further debilitate American security interests. (19) These revelations and more are indicative of the final act of the New Roman Empire reclaiming world dominance through a host of conspirators from within and from without, as was foretold in Daniel 7:23 and reinforced in Revelation 17:9-14.   The original nations that composed the old Roman Empire were broken up many times over the last sixteen centuries, only to reform or die trying in the never-ending quest for empire. Related internal collapse, barbarian invasion, and the natural life and death struggle of a complex civilization invariably lead to old-age, decay, and death. (20) But like the mythical Phoenix rising from the ashes, Rome refuses to die—hence the eternal city and, evidently, eternal empire as well. In more recent times, say the last century, the old Roman Empire was a focal point in two world wars. In WW II, Benito Mussolini represented the Italian component and an infamous Austrian/German by the name of Adolph Hitler picked up where the Carolingian Dynasty and the Habsburg line had disintegrated. The European countries of Germany, France, Spain, Italy, Netherlands, Greece, and Great Britain form the main nucleus of the assembly that comprises the New Roman Empire.

Although the EU is mostly unified through a common passport and currency called the Euro, strangely, Great Britain and the monarchy remain steadfastly protected by the British pound currency. In less than a decade, the Euro currency overtook the U.S. dollar in perceived value. The Euro has an interesting symbol prominent on all currency denominations; that being an outline of the former Roman Empire as a map that is acutely similar to the large reliefs from antiquity prominently displayed in downtown Rome. This is in fact the outline of the core of the New Roman Empire. The Euro may very well be the next world reserve currency. It is currently accepted as readily as American dollars in places like New York, no questions asked. Once the American dollar is internationally renounced and replaced with another reserve currency, the United States will have been subjugated by the E.U. and their fellow world conspirators. The U.S. need not be invaded by any invasion/occupying force, this was proven by the aftermath of the September 11, 2001 terrorist attacks. The travel industry was devastated along with the stock market and peripheral business that drive the U.S., and secondarily world economies.

Imperialism can connote an otherwise repulsive impression throughout a world of sovereign countries and beliefs. The United States was not inclined from its inception with the aspiration or motivation to ultimately become an Imperial power. And although history identifies a contradiction in what is espoused by the U.S. and exemplified in its actions, perception is reality in the divergent myopia of world affairs. Champions of U.S.

diplomatic policy have attempted to downplay American hegemony as being beneficent for the world on multiple levels. The words of "Liberal empire" have been used to describe United States dominance; this cannot neutralize what is implied or known to be part and parcel of Imperial rule. (21) There are some benefits to being friends with the most powerful country extant, and this arrangement is preferable to being resigned to the dark ages without hope or promise. Is America an inadvertent empire? Such a conclusion would tend to downplay what we know of history and how several preceding cultures have influenced the evolution of modern civilization. (22)

The most important geopolitical aspect of a country's existence is in its ability to wage war. Such an imperative invariably compels war instead of peace. The United States has in excess of 650 military bases around the world and in more than 120 countries. Such an extensive reach and worldwide influence is beyond any one industrial enterprise. The implied Imperial overstretch would have to be considered a separate dimension within the boundaries of what constitutes a cohesive world civilization. The United States is the only country to date to have ever successfully attacked an enemy using thermal nuclear weapons. This distinction is a tremendous burden with respect to the invidious antipathy engendered and nurtured by rival nations that desire the spoils of U.S. hegemony. With far-reaching war capabilities, perennial enemies are lurking around every corner. This is what makes the business of warfare money- intensive; a new weapon and correlative support structure are always in need of more of everything. Support industries develop to help the other ancillary components of developing, building, preparing, storing, plotting, spying, and executing war. Consequently, revenue streams evolve to supply graft for politicians and arms dealers that have no better way to earn a constructive living. America has become indispensible in supplying weapon systems not only for its own protection, but also for the next would-be terrorists or opposing player in the "business of war."

The United Nations and the EU know that the absolute control of the world resides in controlling the United States. World trade was not intended to benefit the U.S. but rather provides a host from which the parasites of the world could feed off. Many are from the old world, claiming a unique blood-line that entitles them to an inordinate share of the world. Still others maintain it is the prophecy that must be fulfilled— philosophically or religiously. Based on many antecedents established over centuries, it appears that each competing party has a claim on a mystical and ephemeral vision that was previously awarded by supernatural forces. There have been far too many prophetic pronouncements that have come true with respect to historic world empires living and dying—outside of man's control. (23)

The Barbarians that invade Rome and the surrounding environs in the current time have come to pay tribute and leave offerings of homage and respect. Tourism is an important part of the revenue that the city of Rome has come to accept and enjoy. And although some "indigenous" Romans have found cause to complain about the negative aspect of tourists invading their metropolis, i.e. pollution from tour buses, gawking westerners and crime, they know deep inside that this is Rome as it was intended. As I walked the cobblestone streets of the eternal city, I was struck by the relentless stream of tourists pouring into the city at all hours of the day and night and from every corner of the globe. My hotel was near the main train station, *Roma Termini,* and to watch the incoming tourists lugging their bags and following a map trying to find their accommodations and taking in the sights, all at the same time, were images that left an indelible imprint on my consciousness. I took great pleasure in my first day upon arrival, with wide eyes and the air of mystery that is in every facet of the city. Rome is statistically the number one or two tourist destination in Europe, positioned in between Paris and London in alternating popularity. My expectations were immensely exceeded and even with the sometimes jaded response by some taxi drivers, shop keepers, and restaurant staff, I found myself enthralled by not just the historical artifacts, but also by a spirit that seemed to permeate all aspects of the theatre that is Rome.

I would like to say my favorite historical object/ attraction was the Coliseum or the Vatican, but it seems the Roman people left the most endearing impression on me. Every interaction or simple task was like a production. Unfolding dramas were everywhere, and I had to learn to allow for at least two hours minimum in order to get a good dinner at almost all of the restaurants. A unique culture to be sure and I believe proud of its ancient heritage, even if slightly overshadowed by the events of World War II. I spoke with my tour guide about her recollections of being taught Italian history growing up as a girl. Ila confided in me that she was uncomfortable talking about Mussolini and that her parents taught her to forget that aspect of Italian history and focus on the positive facets that Rome and Italy have contributed to the world throughout history and in totality. (24) An especially unique perspective given to me was the premise of the Italian culture being guilty of an imperious indolence whereby "other people(s) are encouraged to do the heavy lifting." The new barbarians are a testament to the ideal and latent spirit of ancient Rome; the conquered, knowingly or not, perpetuate the continuing legacy of Rome, the eternal empire.

Archaeology continues to add new and diverse knowledge courtesy of the Roman Empire. In London, England a unique Roman gladiator cemetery was discovered in 2003 and continues to yield valuable information about our text-book Empire and its far-flung influences. (25) In southwest England, a large cache of Roman coins was discovered, further revealing the importance of Britannia as a Roman province as late as 224 A.D. (26) Unlike the insular finds of other archaeologically studied cultures, dynasties, and empires, the Roman imperative spans over vast distances. From Pergamum and Constantinople (Istanbul) to the far reaches of the northern British Isles and even Africa. Far beyond these examples, the references previously denoted and outlined clearly speak to the pervasiveness of the Roman-world heritage, a legacy that was preordained in an ancient book known as the Bible—and that book remains indisputable.

NOTES

Drugstore 9000

1. Ancient Roman Medicine: http://www.mmdtkw.org/ VRomanMedicine2002.html
2. Cornelius Celsus: http://www.faqs.org/health/bios/65/Aulus-Cornelius-Celsus.html
3. Eustace Mullins, *Murder by Injection* (Staunton, VA: The National Council for Medical Research, 1995), 3.
4. Howard Wolinsky and Tom Brune, *The Serpent on The Staff: The Unholy Politics of the American Medical Association* (New York: G.P. Putnam's Sons, 1994), 45, 46.
5. American Medical Association: http://www.naturalnews.com/2023195_the_AMA_American_Medical 5/08/2008
6. Ibid.
7. Wolinsky and Brune, 48.
8. Ibid, 75-81.
9. "Pfizer to buy Wyeth for $68 billion," http://www.Reuters.com/articlePrint?ID=USTRE50M1AQ20090126
10. "Merck/Schering-Plough merger would create second-largest drug company," http://www.pbs.org/newshour/updates/health/jan-june09merck_03-09.html
11. Kurt Link, M.D., *The Vaccine Controversy: The History, Use, and Safety of Vaccines.* (Westport, CT: Praeger Publishers, 2005), 91-93.
12. Link, 29, 30.
13. Ibid, 28-31.

14. Leonard G. Horowitz, "Contaminated Vaccines Threaten Public Health," in *Vaccinations,* ed. Mary E. Williams (Farmington Hills, MI: Green Haven Press, 2005), 42-48.

15. Link, 47.

16. "HPV shot found safe, but some experts question its benefits," http://www.cnn.com/2009/HEALTH/08/18/hpv.vaccine.safety/

17. "Medical Groups Promoted HPV Vaccine Using Drug Company Money," http://www.washingtonpost.com/wp-dyn/content/article/2009/08/18/AR2009081802499

18. JAMA: "Gardasil safe, but promos questionable," http://www.fiercepharma.com/node/11506/print "FDA approves Merck's Gardasil for boys," http://www.google.com

19. Randall Neustaedter, OMD, *The Vaccine Guide: Risks and Benefits for Children and Adults.* (Berkeley, CA: North Atlantic Books, 2002), 48.

20. Barbara Loe. Fisher, "Parents Should Be Allowed to Opt Out of Vaccinating Their Children," in *Vaccinations,* ed. Mary E. Williams (Farmington Hills, MI: Green Haven Press, 2005), 54-64.

21. Neustaedter, 74-76.

22. Ibid, 276.

23. "Walgreen", http://en.wikipedia.org/wiki/Walgreens & "CVS pharmacy," http://en.wikipedia.org/wiki/CVS/pharmacy & "Rite Aid," http://en.wikipedia.org/wiki/Rite_Aid & "Wal-Mart, Your Friendly Drugstore," http://www.businessweek.com/bwdaily/dnflash/content/jun2008/db2008064_545169.htm

24. "CVS sued by Texas for illegally dumping patient information," http://en.wikipedia.org/wiki/CVS/pharmacy

25. Ibid.

26. "Government moves to staunch massive Medicare fraud," http://in.reuters.com/articlePrint?ID=INTRE5604FL20090701

27. Shannon Brownlee, "Why Does Health Care Cost So Much?" *AARP Magazine*, July/August 2008, 50.

28. Aldous Huxley, *Brave New World (Revisited)* (New York: Harper & Brothers, 1958). Original version written 1932.

29. "Antidepressant Use Nearly Doubles," http://www.webmd.

com/depression/news/20090803/antidepressant-use-nearly-doubles

30. Bertrand Russell, *The Impact Of Science On Society* (New York: AMS Press, 1968), 50.

31. "The Caduceus versus the Staff of Asclepius," http://www.drblayney.com/Asclepius.html

Buy Some Money

1. Joe Dominguez and Vickie Robin, *Your Money or Your Life* (New York: Penguin Books, 1992), 54.

2. Marie Bussing – Burks, *Influential Economists* (Minneapolis, MN: The Oliver Press Inc, 2003), 29.

3. Eustace Mullins, *The World Order: Our Secret Rulers* (Staunton, VA: Ezra Pound Institute of Civilization, 1992), 6.

4. Ibid, 9.

5. William Cooper, *Behold a Pale Horse* (Sedona, AZ: Light Technology Publishing, 1991), 41.

6. Ibid, 42.

7. Texe Marrs, *Circle of Intrigue* (Austin TX: Living Truth Publishers, 1995), 242.

8. Benjamin Franklin (Funk & Wagnalls New Encyclopedia, Volume 11, 1986 edition), p 20.

9. "List of Freemasons" (Ben Franklin) http://en.wikipedia.org/wiki/List_of_Freemasons (accessed September 23, 2009).

10. *Rome: Rise And Fall Of An Empire* producer, Robert Gardner, writer, Carrie Gardner, directed by, Leif Anders, 611 min., A & E Television Networks, History, 2008, DVD.

11. Eustace Mullins, *The Secrets of the Federal Reserve* (Staunton, VA: Bankers Research Institute, 1993), 1.

12. Gary H. Kah, *En Route to Global Occupation* (Lafayette LA: Hunting House Publishers, 1992), 88.

13. Ibid, 107.

14. Ibid, 28.

15. Jason Goodwin, *Greenback: The Almighty Dollar and the Invention of America* (New York: Henry Holt and Company, LLC, 2003), 102.

16. Donald B. Cole, *The Presidency of Andrew Jackson* (Lawrence KS: University Press of Kansas, 1993), 155.

17. Ibid, 187.

18. "Andrew Jackson" http://en.wikipedia.org/wiki/Andrew_Jackson (accessed October 7, 2009).

19. Kah, 28-29.

20. Donald R. Wells, *The Federal Reserve System: A History* (North Carolina: McFarland & Company, Inc., Publishers, 2004), 12.

21. Ibid, 16.

22. Mullins, *Secrets*, 7.

23. Ibid, 11.

24. "Paulson Threatened Great Depression, Food Riots To Get Bailout Bill Passed" http://www.propagandamatrix.com/articles/july2009/071709_food_riots.htm (accessed October 11, 2009).

25. *Wall Street*, produced by Edward Pressman, written by Stanley Weiser & Oliver Stone, and directed by Oliver Stone, 126 min., Twentieth Century Fox, 1987, DVD.

26. Gardner, *Rome: The Rise And Fall Of An Empire*, The Invasion of Britain.

27. "London," http://en.wikipedia.org/wiki/London (accessed September 29, 2009).

28. E.C. Knuth, *The Empire Of "The City"* (San Diego CA: The Book Tree, 2006), 7.

29. Ibid, 12-15.

30. "London," http://en.wikipedia.org/wiki/London

31. Mullins, *Secrets*, 63-65.

32. David Gould, *"What It Is All About!"* http://www.no-debts.com/theseries/1index.txt (accessed October 11, 2009), p 14.

33. Ibid, 17.

34. Ibid, 24. The * = National Debt Clock Real Time @ http://www.usdebtclock.org/

35. Gould, *"Slavery"* http://www.no-debts.com/theseries/1index.txt (accessed October 11, 2009), 8.

36. Carroll Quigley, *Tragedy & Hope: A History of The World in Our Time* (New York: The Macmillan Company, 1966), pp 324-329.

37. Ibid, 325.

38. Niall Ferguson, *The Ascent of Money: A Financial History of The World* (New York: The Penguin Press, 2008), 106.

39. Inhofe: "Roll Back the Bailout" http://inhofe.senate.gov/public/index.cfm?FuseAction=PressRoom.PressReleases&Conte see also "Inhofe: No Way Of Knowing Where Bailout Money Has Gone" http://www.prisonplanet.com/inhofe-no-way-of-knowing (accessed October 14, 2009).

40. "Ron Paul Introduced Audit the Fed Bill in 1983-Both Parties Blocked It for More Than 25 Years http://georgewashington2.blogspot.com/2009/09/ron-paul-introduced-audit-fed-bill-in.html (accessed October 16, 2009).

41. "Report: Regulator was tipped off about Madoff fraud as early as 1992" http://www.guardian.co.uk/business (accessed September 02, 2009). Also see "Madoff documents reveal incredulous, unfocused SEC" http://www.reuters.com 10/31/2009

42. Bryan Burrough, "Marc Dreier's Crime of Destiny," *Vanity Fair*, November 2009, 184.

43. "Goldman defector draws attention to electronic trading firms" http://cnnmoney. See Goldman/electronic trading. (accessed July 28, 2009).

44. "Senator Schumer Calls for Ban on Flash Orders" http://www.advancedtrading.com. See Schumer/ ban flash orders. (accessed July 28, 2009).

45. Robert B. Reich, *Supercapitalism: the transformation of business, democracy, and everyday life* (New York: Alfred A. Knopf, 2007), 12.

46. Ibid, 71.

47. Ibid, pp 131, 158, 166.

48. Peter Heather, *The Fall of the Roman Empire: A New History of Rome and the Barbarians* (New York: Oxford University Press, 2006), 110.

49. Ibid, 120.

Blood for Oil

1. Jeremy Rifkin, *The Hydrogen Economy* (New York: Jeremy P. Tarcher/Penguin, 2002), 62.
2. Kenneth S. Deffeyes, *Beyond Oil: The View from Hubbert's Peak* (New York: Hill and Wang, 2005), 40.
3. Michael T. Klare, *Blood and oil: the dangers and consequences of America's growing petroleum dependency* (New York: Metropolitan Books Henry Holt and Company, LLC, 2004), 28.
4. Ibid, 30.
5. Ibid, 39.
6. Ibid, 35.
7. Peter Calvocoressi, *World politics since 1945* (New York: Longman Inc, 1982), 251.
8. Ibid, 252.
9. Klare, 40, 41.
10. Ibid, 46.
11. Webster G. Tarpley and Anton Chaitkin, *George Bush: The Unauthorized Biography* (Joshua Tree, CA: Progressive Press, 2008), 564-567.
12. Ibid, 625.
13. Klare, 113.
14. Ibid, 56-58.
15. Ibid, 67.
16. James Perloff, *The Shadows Of Power* (Appleton, WI: Western Islands, 1988), 256.
17. Ibid, 154.
18. Ibid, 158.
19. Ibid, 155. *Between Two Ages*
20. Daniel Estulin, *The True Story of The Bilderberg Group* (Walterville, OR: TrineDay LLC, 2009), 322.
21. Zbigniew Brzezinski, *The grand chessboard: American primacy and its geostrategic imperatives* (New York: Basic Books, 1997), 194.
22. Ibid, 53.
23. Jon Rosenwasser, "The Bush Administration's Doctrine of Preemption (and Prevention): When, How, Where?" *Council on*

Foreign Relations (2004), http://www.cfr.org/publication/6799/bush_administrations_doctrine_of_preemption

24. "Gulf War oil spill" http://en.wikipedia.org/wiki/Gulf_oil_spill (accessed December 2, 2009).

25. "Kuwait oil fires" http://en.wikipedia.org/wiki/Kuwati_oil_fires (accessed December 2, 2009). See also - Colin Campbell, two billion barrels estimated loss, pg 98.

26. Toby Harnden, "Bin Laden is wanted: dead or alive, says Bush" http://www.telegraph.co.uk/news/worldnews/asia/afghanistan/1340895/Bin-Laden

27. Michael C. Ruppert, *Crossing The Rubicon: The Decline Of The American Empire At The End Of The Age Of Oil* (Gabriola Island, BC Canada: New Society Publishers, 2004), 123. See also, "Osama bin Laden Killed 'Justice is Done,' President Says," ABC News by Dean Schabner and Karen Travers http://abcnews.go.com/Blotter/osama-bin-laden-killed/story

28. Ibid, 127.

29. Ibid, 128.

30. Klare, 19.

31. Ruppert, 20.

32. Ibid, 535.

33. Ibid, 69.

34. "Cheney's Halliburton stock options rose 3,281% last year, senator finds" http://www.rawstory.com/news/2005/Cheneys_stock_options_rose_3281_last_1011.html (accessed March 6, 2009). See also "Halliburton Makes a Killing on Iraq War" http://www.corpwatch.org/article.php?id=6008 (accessed December 10, 2009).

35. Ibid.

36. Rifkin, 73.

37. Deffeyes, 5.

38. D. Stan Jones, *Elements of Petroleum Processing* (Chichester, West Sussex, England: John Wiley & Sons Ltd, 1995), 6.

39. Tim Appenzeller, "The End of Cheap Oil," *National Geographic*, June 2004, 82.

40. Ibid, 83.

41. Bill D. Berger and Kenneth E. Anderson, Ph.D., *Modern Petroleum: A Basic Primer of the Industry* (Tulsa, OK: PennWell Publishing Company, 1992), 21-26.

42. Ibid, 46, 47.
43. Charles F. Conaway, *The Petroleum Industry: A Non technical Guide* (Tulsa, OK: PennWell Publishing Company, 1999), 24.
44. C.J. (Colin) Campbell, *Oil Crises* (Brentwood, Essex, United Kingdom: Multi-Science Publishing Co. Ltd, 2005), 44, 45.
45. Berger and Anderson, 136-138. Also, Deepwater Horizon oil spill http://en.wikipedia.org/wiki/Deepwater_Horizon_oil_spill
46. Jessica Williams, *50 Facts That Should Change The World* (New York: The Disinformation Company Ltd, 2007), 151-154.
47. Rifkin, 89.
48. Campbell, 57, 58.
49. Joan Ogden and Daniel Sperling, "The Hope for Hydrogen," in *U.S. National Debate Topic 2008-2009: Alternative Energy 80:03,* ed. Paul McCaffrey (New York: The H.W. Wilson Company, 2008), 115, 116.
50. "Gas Price Historical Price Charts" http://gasbuddy.com/gb_retail_price_chart.aspx
51. Ruth Mantell, "Gas prices at record high, holiday travel down," July 5, 2008. http://www.marketwatch.com/story (accessed December 9, 2009).
52. Keith Naughton, "Should You Pay $6 Per Gallon?" *Newsweek,* April 25, 2008. http://www.newsweek.com/id/133994
53. Campbell, 25.
54. Ibid, 91.
55. *Alternative Energy,* 135.
56. Ibid, 138.
57. Cullen Murphy, *Are We Rome? the fall of an empire and the fate of America* (New York: First Mariner Books, 2007), 24.
58. Joseph A. Tainter, *The Collapse of Complex Societies* (Cambridge UK: Cambridge University Press, 1988), 23, 26, 27.
59. Murphy, 36.
60. Rifkin, 58.
61. *Rome: Rise And Fall Of An Empire* (Julius Caesar). See also, (The Puppet Master).
62. Tainter, 140-143.
63. Murphy, 71.
64. Tim Appenzeller, 89.
65. Robert Longley, "Illegal Immigration Costs California Over

Ten Billion Annually," *About.com Guide,* http://usgovinfo. about.com/od/immigrationnaturalization/a/caillegals (accessed December 29, 2009). See also, Federation For American Immigration Reform http://www.fairus.org/site/ News

66. Frosty Wooldridge, "Stopping Illegal Immigration: California Border Initiative" http://www.newswithviews.com/ Wooldridge/frosty88.htm (accessed 12-29-2009).

67. Paul Harris, "Will California become America's first failed state?" *The Observer,* Sunday 4 October 2009, http://www. guardian.co.uk/world/2009/oct/04/california-failing-state-debt (accessed October 09, 2009).

68. Shane Goldmacher and Evan Halper, "Schwarzenegger to seek federal help for California budget" *L A Times,* http://www. latimes.com/news/local/la-me-budget23-2009dec23 See also, Stu Woo and Jim Carlton, "California Requests Billions From U.S." http://online.wsj.com/article/SB126297948893221947. html January 09, 2010.

Sun Touch

1. Ben Lieberman, "Beware of Cap and Trade Climate Bills" http://www.heritage.org/Research/Economy/wml723.cfm

2. Kenneth R. Lang, *Sun, earth and sky* (New York: Springer Science + Business Media, LLC, 2006), 29.

3. Linda T. Elkins-Tanton, *The Sun, Mercury, and Venus* (New York: Chelsea House Publishers, 2006), 52.

4. Ibid, 24. (Note: although most solar physicists estimate the time needed for the energy to travel from the core through the sun to the surface at 170,000 years, there are some estimates as low as 100,000 years: Leon Golub & Jay M. Pasachoff, *Nearest star: the surprising science of our sun* (Cambridge, MA: Harvard University Press, 2001), 51.

5. The Living Bible, paraphrased: Ecclesiastes, chapter 2, verse 17 & chapter 4, verse 16.

6. Elkins-Tanton, 82-133.

7. Ibid, 191.

8. Lang, 23.

9. Elkins-Tanton, 44.

10. Michael J. Carlowicz and Ramon E. Lopez, *Storms from the*

sun: the emerging science of space weather (Washington, DC: The Joseph Henry Press, 2002), 8, 98.

11. Richard W. Noone, *5/5/2000: Ice: the ultimate disaster.* (New York: Three Rivers Press, 1982), 310-321.

12. Lang, 227-229.

13. Ibid, 37.

14. Jonathan Leake, "World may not be warming, say scientists" http://www.timesonline.co.uk/tol/news/environment/article7026317.ece (accessed February 13, 2010). See also, Resolving the Global Warming Fraud http://hotair/greenroom/archives/2010/02/12/resolving-the-global-warming-fraud

15. "Solar Energy" http://en.wikipedia.org/wiki/Solar_energy#Energy_from_the_Sun (accessed February 05, 2010).

16. Leon Golub & Jay M. Pasachoff, *Nearest star: the surprising science of our sun* (Cambridge, MA: Harvard University Press, 2001), 12.

17. "5 Billion Worldwide Mobile Subscriptions in 2010" http://www.techtree.com/India/News/5_Billion_Worldwide_Mobile_Subscriptions (accessed February 26, 2010).

18. Larry Spargimino, "Suddenly No More Time" *Prophetic Observer* June 2003-Vol. 10, No. 6 L-962 http://www.swrc.com

19. Larry Borsato, "Information overload on the Web, and searching for the right sifting tool" http://www.thestandard.com/news/2008/08/28/knowledge-doubling-curve (accessed February 26, 2010).

20. Travis Bradford, *Solar revolution: the economic transformation of the global energy industry* (Cambridge, MA: The MIT Press, 2006), 101.

21. *Rome: Rise And Fall Of An Empire* producer, Robert Gardner, writer, Carrie Gardner, directed by, Leif Anders, 611 min., A & E Television Networks, History, 2008, DVD. (The Soldiers' Emperor – Aurelian)

22. Adrian Gilbert and Maurice Cotterell, *The Mayan Prophecies: unlocking the secrets of a lost civilization* (New York: Barnes & Noble, Inc., 1996), 183.

23. Ibid, 244-253.

24. Maurice Cotterell, *The Tutankhamun prophecies: the sacred*

secrets of the Mayas, Egyptians, and Freemasons (Rochester, VT: Bear & Company, 2001), 277.

25. Gilbert, 179-183.
26. Malcolm Gladwell, *Outliers: the story of success* (New York: Little Brown and Company, 2008), 61, 62.
27. Cotterell, 258.
28. Gladwell, 65-68.
29. Cotterell, 258. (In reference to record births): Mike Stobbe "A good year for babies" http://www.redlandsdailyfacts.com/news/ci_12195230 (accessed April 24, 2009).

More Bread and Circuses

1. Michael Kerrigan, *A Dark History: The Roman Emperors* (New York: Metro Books, 2008), 178.
2. Roman Circus Maximus (building) http://en.wikipedia.org/wiki/Circus_(building) (accessed May 9, 2010).
3. Ultimate Fighter Championship (B.J. Penn verses Joe Stevenson) http://www.spike.com/BJPenn (graphic bloody violence).
4. Nate Penn, "I Like to Punish People," *Maxim*, June 2009, 92.
5. Dan Reilly, "Teenager Sends Over 14,000 Text Messages in One Month," http://switched.com/2009/01/13/teenager-sends-over-14-000-text-messages-in-one
6. Daniel Long, "College duo's text messaging record blunder nets them US $26,000 bill," http://www.pcauthority.com.au/News/143183,college-duos-text-messaging-record-blunder... (accessed April 23, 2009).
7. Eric Chabrow, "Spying on Facebook," http://www.govinfosecurity.com/p_print.php (accessed December 30, 2009).
8. Jeremy A. Kaplan, "The FBI Knows Where You Are, Thanks to Your Cell Phone," http://www.foxnews.com/scitech/tech/ci.The+FBI+Knows+Where+You+Are (accessed February 12, 2010).
9. Lance Whitney, "Cell phone subscriptions to hit 5 billion globally," http://reviews.cnet.com/8301-13970_7-10454065-78.html (accessed June 6, 2010).
10. Ibid.

11. Brent Whiting, "Police: Text messaging to blame for fatal accident," http://www.azcentral.com/community/peoria/articles/0831gl-peofatal0813.html See also, Bret Schulte, "Outlawing Text Messaging While Driving Legislators in several states respond to safety concerns" http://www.usnews.com/articles/news/national/2008/02/11/outlawing-text-messaging

12. "Wipeout," Wipeout on TV, *Wipeout Blind Date* http://www.tv.com/wipeout/show/75217/summary.html (accessed June 18, 2010).

13. Breeanna Hare, "Death of Wipeout contestant under investigation," http://www.cnn.com/2009/SHOWBIZ/TV/11/12/tom.sparks.death.wipeout/index.html

14. Radio Business Report/Television Business Report – Voice of the Broadcasting Industry. "ABC wins the week in total viewers," Wipeout-Tues. http://www.rbr.com/tv-cable_ratings/24862.html

15. Steven Fife, "CBS Confirms Survivor 20: Heroes Vs. Villains - Tenth Anniversary Season To Bring Back Show's Biggest Stars Ever," http://reality-tv-suite101.com/article.cfm/survivor_20_looks_to_be_heroes_vs_villians See also, Survivor (U.S. TV series). http://en.wikipedia.org/wiki/Survivor_(U.S._TV_series)

16. "Avatar left film reviewer feeling sick," http://uk.movies.yahoo.com/blog/article/9633/avatar-left-film-reviewer-feeling-sick-html

17. Dr. Nick Begich, *Controlling the Human Mind* (Anchorage, AK: Earthpulse Press, 2006), 127.

18. Ibid, 38, 71, 98. See also, David G. Myers, *Exploring Psychology* (New York: Worth Publishers, 2009), 181-183.

19. Evan S. Benn, "Seeing Triple at the 3-D Movie?," http://www.baltimoresun.com/health/sns-health-3-d-movie-sickness,0,4990238.story

20. Joseph A. Tainter, *The Collapse of Complex Societies* (Cambridge UK: Cambridge University Press, 1988), 126, 129, 132.

21. Bloomberg News | June 3, 2010 "More than 40m now use food stamps," http://www.boston.com/news/nation/articles/2010/06/03/more_than_40m_use_food

22. Kerrigan, 33.

23. Peter G. Peterson, *Running On Empty* (New York: Farrar, Straus and Giroux, 2004), 57-64.

24. Ibid, 170, 171.

25. Social Security (United States) http://en.wikipedia.org/wiki/Social_Security_Act

26. United States Debt Clock – http://usdebtclock.org

27. St. Valentine's Day Ideas, Facts and Fun, http://www.theromantic.com/valentinesday/main.htm

28. Ibid.

29. Norman Herr, PH.D., Television & Health, http://www.csun.edu/science/health/docs/tv&health.html

30. David Liu, "Childhood obesity on the rise in the U.S." http://www.foodconsumer.org/newsite/Non-food/Lifestyle/american_children_obese (accessed July 24, 2010).

31. Dan S. Wilson, 'Childhood Diabetes", http://ezinearticles.com/?Childhood-Diabetes&id=2544163 See also, Christine Cadena, "Risks of Coronary Heart Disease in Children", http://www.associatedcontent.com/article/180292/risks_of_coronary_heart_

32. Herr.

33. "Toddler may have shot, killed 9-year-old brother in Florence", *Central/Southern Arizona News.* http://www.abc15.com/content/news/centralsoutharizona/story/Toddler-may-have-shot-

34. "Teen says he drowned 4-year-old to protect secret, police say", CNN.com, http://cnn.site.printthis.clickability.com/pt/cpt?action=cpt&title=Teen+says+he+drowned

35. Samuel Goldsmith, "Boy who shot dad's fiancée got gun as Christmas present", http://www.nydailynews.com/news/2009/02/22/2009-02-22_boy_who_shot_dads_ See also, "Attorney for Boy Murder Suspect: Move Case to Juvenile Court", *Fox News* http://www.foxnews.com/story/0,2933,498384,00.html

36. David Lieb and Chris Blank, "Mo. Teen to be tried as adult in death of girl, 9", The *Associated Press*, http://www.google.com/hostednews/ap/article/AleqM5j0daWk3srlz (accessed November 18, 2009).

37. Felicia Fonseca, "Plea deal for boy, 9, who killed dad,

roommate", *Associated Press*, http://www.sfgate.com/cgi-bin/article.cgi?f=/c/a/2009/02/19/MNCE16160N.DTL

38. Caesarean section, http://en.wikipedia.org/wiki/Caesarean_section
39. Ibid.
40. Denise Grady, "New Guidelines Seek to Reduce Rate of Repeat Caesareans", *The New York Times*, http://www.nytimes.com/2010/07/22/health/22birth.html
41. Caesarean section. See also, Steven Reinberg "C-Section Rate in U.S. Climbs to All-Time High: Report" MSN Health. http://health.msn.com/pregnancy/articlepage,aspx
42. Kerrigan, 95.
43. Nero, http://en.wikipedia.org/wiki/Nero

The Philosophy of Truth

1. Dave Robinson and Judy Groves, *Introducing Philosophy* (Australia: McPherson's Printing Group, 1999), 14.
2. James Mannion, *Essentials of Philosophy* (New York: Fall River Press, 2006), 16.
3. Robinson and Groves, 5, 12.
4. Paul Strathern, *Plato in 90 Minutes* (Chicago IL: Ivan R. Dee, 1996), 19.
5. David G. Myers, *Exploring Psychology* (New York: Worth Publishers, 2009), 138-143.
6. Strathern, *Plato*, 35.
7. Paul Strathern, *Aristotle in 90 Minutes* (Chicago IL: Ivan R. Dee, 1996), 25.
8. Strathern, *Aristotle*, 19.
9. Mannion, 39.
10. Augustine of Hippo, http://en.wikipedia.org/wiki/Saint_Augustine
11. Romans chapter 13: 13-14.
12. Matthew 16: 18 "And I also say to you that you are Peter, and upon this rock I will build My church; and the gates of Hades shall not overpower it," NIV
13. Elaine Pagels, *The Gnostic Gospels* (New York: Vintage Books, 1989), xxi-xxiii
14. Ibid, 36, 94-95.

15. Benedict of Nursia, http://en.wikipedia.org/wiki/Saint_Benedict

16. Ibid.

17. Thomas Cahill, *Mysteries of the Middle Ages* (New York: Anchor Books, 2006), 69.

18. Ibid, 57.

19. History of the Catholic Church, http://en.wikipedia.org/wiki/History_of_Catholic_Church

20. John Dowling, *The History Of Romanism From The Earliest Corruptions Of Christianity To The Present Time* (New York: Edward Fuller, 1845), 60-64.

21. Derek A. Wilson, *Charlemagne* (New York: Doubleday, 2006), 32-35.

22. Ibid, 76.

23. Pope Saint Leo III, http://en.wikipedia.org/wiki/Pope_Leo_III

24. Wilson, 81, 82.

25. Ibid, 2.

26. List of Catholic Colleges and Universities, http://www.stireness.org/information/college_list,html

27. Top Catholic Colleges and Universities, http://www.go4ivy.com/catholic.asp

28. Early Middle Ages, http://en.wikipedia.org/wiki/Early_Middle_Ages

29. Ibid.

30. Saint Dominic, http://en.wikipedia.org/wiki/Saint_Dominic

31. Saint Thomas Aquinas, http://en.wikipedia.org/wiki/Saint_Thomas_Aquinas

32. Cahill, 215.

33. Saint Thomas Aquinas.

34. Ibid.

35. Matt Slick, Why is it necessary to write about Roman Catholicism? http://carm.org/why-it-necessary-write-about-roman-catholicism

36. Cistercians (Funk & Wagnalls New Encyclopedia, Volume 6, 1986 edition), p 302.

37. Edward Burman, *The Templars Knights Of God* (Rochester VT: Destiny Books, 1986) 26-28.

38. Sharan Newman, *The Real History Behind the Templars* (New York: The Berkeley Publishing Group, 2007), 265-267, 280.
39. Ibid, 193, 195.
40. Ibid. 156, 160.
41. Burman, 28, 29.
42. Newman, 158.
43. Dowling, 324, 325.
44. Steven Sora, *The Lost Treasure of The Knights Templar* (Rochester VT: Destiny Books, 1999). See also, D'Arcy O'Conner, *The Secret Treasure of Oak Island.*
45. List of largest church buildings in the world, http://en.wikipedia.org/wiki/List_of_largest_church_buildings_in_the_world
46. *Rome From Its Origins To The Present Time,* (Rome: LOZZI ROMA S.A.S, 2005), 88. [ISBN 978-88-86843-01-0]
47. Robinson and Groves, 50.
48. Paul Strathern, *Machiavelli in 90 Minutes* (Chicago, IL: Ivan R. Dee, 1998), 36-39.
49. Ibid, 47.
50. Ibid, 77.
51. Martin Luther, http://en.wikipedia.org/wiki/Martin_Luther Note: bible verses Ephesians 2: 8-9 " For it is by grace you have been saved, through faith---and this not from yourselves, it is the gift of God---not by works, so that no one can boast." NIV See also, Romans 3: 27-28.
52. Ibid.
53. 1 John 4 verse 7. And special note verse 20, "If anyone says "I love God" but keeps on hating his brother, he is a liar; for if he doesn't love his brother who is right there in front of him, how can he love God whom he has never seen?" NIV
54. Robinson and Groves, 78.
55. A.R. Lacey, *A Dictionary Of Philosophy* (New York: Barnes & Noble Books, 1999), 138.
56. Glass-Steagall Act (Banking Act of 1933) http://en.wikipedia.org/wiki/Glass-Steagall_Act See also, *Inside Job,* produced, written, and directed by Charles Ferguson, 109 min., Sony Pictures Classics, 2010, DVD.
57. Howard P. Kainz, *G.W.F. Hegel: The Philosophical System* (New York: Twayne Publishers, 1996), 151.
58. Robinson and Groves, 76.

59. Age of Enlightenment (Important figures)
60. http://en.wikipedia.org/wiki/Enlightenment_Era
61. Ninian Smart, *Worldviews, Crosscultural Explorations of Human Beliefs* (New Jersey: Prentice-Hall, Inc. 2000), 105.
62. Mannion, 126.
63. Kathy Lynn Grossman, "Most religious groups in USA have lost ground, survey finds" *USA Today* http://www.usatoday.com/news/religion/2009-03-09-american-religion-ARIS See also, "America becoming less Christian, survey finds" http://cnn.site. CNN.com
64. "Thou shalt shoplift, priest tells congregation" http://www.msnbc.msn.com/id34522514/ns/world_news-world_faith/ (accessed 12/22/2009).
65. Michael Paulson, "Robinson elevated as first gay bishop Ovations, protests greet Episcopal ceremony in N.H." *The Boston Globe*, November 3, 2003. http://www.boston.com/news/local/new_hampshire/articles/2003/11/03/robinson_elevated See also, "Episcopal Church consecrates first openly lesbian bishop" By the CNN Wire Staff. http://cnn.site. CNN.com
66. Michael Barbaro and David W. Chen, "Bloomberg Sets Record for His Own Spending on Elections" *The New York Times*, October 24, 2009. http://www.nytimes.com/2009/10/24/nyregion/24mayor.html See also, Colleen Long, "NYC mayor spent record $102M to win 3rd term" *The Associated Press*, accessed 11/27/2009.
67. Ken McLaughlin, "Meg Whitman writes $20 million check to campaign, bringing total to $91 million." *The Mercury News*, 6/15/2010. http://www.mercurynews.com
68. See also, Phillip Caulfield, "Meg Whitman's Money Couldn't Buy an Election." *Dailey News*, November 3, 2010. http://www.usnews.com/news/articles/2010/11/03/meg-whitmans-money-couldnt-buy-an-election See also, Maeve Reston, "Boxer not only beat Fiorina, she outspent her," *Los Angeles Times*, December 03, 2010.
69. Z. Byron Wolf, "Ethics Committee Probes Countrywide Loans for Senators." http://blogs.abcnews.com/thenote/2009/07/ethics-committee-probes-countrywide-loans See also, Larry Margasak, "Dozens of House Members scrutinized, report

shows." *The Associated Press*, 10/30/2009. See also, James C. McKinley Jr. "Ex-House Leader Delay Found Guilty in Texas Case." *The New York Times,* November 24, 2010. http://www.nytimes.com Also, "Texas jury convicts Tom Delay" http://content.usatoday.com/communities/onpolitics/post/2010/11/tom-delay-trial-money Also, Paul Courson, "Louisiana ex-congressman gets 13 years on corruption conviction" CNN. Com. http://cnn.site. Also, Alex M. Parker, "A Lonely Guilty Verdict for Charlie Rangel." (House committee finds Rep. Charlie Rangel guilty of violating ethics rules and recommends censure). http://politics.usnews.com/news/articles/2010/11/24/

70. Paul Kane and Chris Cillizza, "Sen. Ensign Acknowledges an Extramarital Affair," *The Washington Post,* Wednesday, June 17, 2009. http://www.washingtonpost.com/wp-dyn/content/article/2009/06/16/AR2009061602746 See also, JoAnne Allen, "Nevada senator Ensign resigns under ethics cloud," *Reuters,* Thursday, April 21, 2011. Also, Raymond Hernandez, "New York Congressman Resigns Over E-Mails," *The New York Times,* February 9, 2011. http://www.nytimes.com/2011/0210/us/politics Also, "Congressman Chris Lee Resigns After Shirtless Photo Posted on Internet," By Matthew Jaffe and John Parkinson, February 9, 2011. ABC NEWS/Politics, http://abcnews.go.com/Politics/congressman-chris-lee-resigns-shirtless-photo-posted-inter

71. Also, Michael Barbaro, "Weiner Admits He Sent Lewd Photos; Says He Won't Resign," *The New York Times,* June 6, 2011. Also, Karen Zraick and Andrew Miga, "Defiant no longer, Weiner resigns in sex scandal," *The Associated Press,* June 16, 2011. http://www.sltrib.com/sltrib/world/52018895-68/weiner-york-party-lee.html See also, David Vitter, http://en.wikipedia.org/wiki/David_Vitter (Vitter, the junior Senator from Louisiana, was identified as a client of a prostitution service in July of 2007). Note: other prominent sex scandals include Rep. Mark Foley, Rep. Barney Frank, and former President Bill Clinton (Monica Lewinsky).

72. Liz Sidoti, "Poll: 78 percent don't trust big government," *The Associated Press,* April 18, 2010. http://www.msnbc.msn.com/id36629520/ns/politics/print/1/displaymode/109822

Roman Rule(s)

1. Holy Lance, http://en.wikipedia.org/wiki/Spear_of_Destiny
2. Spear of Destiny, Holy Lance, http://crystalinks.com/speardestiny.html
3. Saint Longinus, http://en.wikipedia.org/wiki/Saint_Longinus See also, Mark 15: 39 and Luke 23: 47
4. The "SPEAR OF DESTINY" http://petragrail.tripod.com/spear.html
5. Spear of Destiny, Holy Lance.
6. Habsburg Monarchy, http://en.wikipedia.org/wiki/Hapsburg_Monarchy
7. Cullen Murphy, *Are We Rome?* (New York: First Mariner Books, 2007), 1. See also, Road, http://en.wikipedia.org/wiki/Road
8. Eric Jaffe, "New Reports: Americans Drove 3 Trillion Miles in 2010" http://www.infrastructurist.com/2011/03/03/news-report-americans-drove-3-trillion-miles
9. Trans-Texas Corridor, http://en.wikipedia.org/wiki/Trans-Texas_Corridor
10. Trans-Texas Corridor NEWS, http://www.transtexascorridor.blogspot.com/
11. *Endgame,* produced, written, and directed by Alex Jones, 140 min., Infowars.com, 2007, DVD.
12. TTC News Archives: "An almost frictionless machine for stripping wealth" http://corridornews.blogspot.com/2010/10/almost-frictionless-machine-for.html
13. Ibid.
14. Judy Lin, "California may borrow in case of federal default" *Associated Press,* 7/13/2011. http://www.mercurynews.com/breaking-news/ci_18471092 See also, David Bailey, "Minnesota budget deal pushes problem down the road" *Reuters,* 7/15/2011. http://www.reuters.com/assets/print See also, Karen Pierog, "Illinois governor signs budget but state's problems mount" *Reuters,* 7/02/2011. http://www.reuters.com/assets/print
15. Terry James, *The American Apocalypse* (Eugene, OR: Harvest House Publishers, 2009), 92, 134, 136.
16. Samuel P. Huntington, *The Clash of Civilizations and the*

Remaking of World Order (New York: Simon & Schuster, 1996), 188, 251.

17. Ibid, 263.

18. James, 210-215. See also, F. William Engdahl, "Collapse of the Greenback? Will the Dollar get an "Arab Oil Shock"? *Money Watch,* October 9, 2009. http://prisonplanet.com/collapse-of-the-greenback-will-the-dollar-get-an See also, "US government loses triple-A credit rating" MSNBC. Com 8/06/2011. http://www.msnbc.msn.com/id/44040574/ns/business-stocks

19. Walter Brandimarte and Melanie Lee, "China tells U.S. 'good old days' of borrowing are over" *The Associated Press,* August 06, 2011. http://www.theglobeandmail.com/news/asia-pacific/china-tells-us-good-old-days-of-b... See also, Thomas Mucha, "Who owns America? Hint: It's not China" *Global Post,* July 22, 2011. (http://www.businessinsider.com/who-owns-us-debt-2011-7#)

20. Joseph A. Tainter, *The Collapse of Complex Societies* (Cambridge UK: Cambridge University Press, 1988), 76-77.

21. Robert Dujarric and William E. Odom, *America's Inadvertent Empire* (New Haven CT: Yale University Press, 2004), 40.

22. Ibid, 209.

23. Romans 13: 1-2 "Obey the government, for God is the one that has put it there. There is no government anywhere that God has not placed in power." And, Daniel 4: 7 "the most high dominates the kingdoms of this world, and gives them to anyone he wants, even the lowliest of men." And, Zechariah 12: 3 "Jerusalem will be a heavy stone burdening the world. And though all the nations of the earth unite in an attempt to move her, they will all be crushed." And, Jeremiah 30: 1-3, 31: 35-36. Note: the prophecies relative to the Israelites are irrefutable. (The United States is attached to Israel through supernatural decree and will serve Gods prophetic purpose inexorably.) NIV

24. Personal informal interview with Ila (pronounced EE-La) transpired in Rome on September 13, 2010.

25. "Roman gladiator cemetery found in England" the CNN Wire Staff 6/07/2010. http://www.cnn.com/2010/WORLD/europe/06/07/england.roman.cemetery/

26. Chris Hellier "Roman Coin Cache Discovered" Archaeology

http://www.archaeology.org/0003/newsbriefs/coins.html
See also, "Hoard of 52,500 Roman Coins Discovered Near
Frome by Metal Detectorist" Heritage Key 07/08/2010.
http://heritage-key.com/blogs/bija/hoard-52500-roman-coins-discovered-near-frome-metal

www.ingramcontent.com/pod-product-compliance
Lightning Source LLC
Chambersburg PA
CBHW061302280526
45784CB00002B/860